ENGLISH SLANG AND COLLOQUIALISMS

ENGLISH SLANG AND COLLOQUIALISMS

Josna Sebastian

Commonwealth

English Slang and Colloquialisms

Edition : 2024

ISBN 978-81-311-0244-2

Published by :

COMMONWEALTH PUBLISHERS
4831/24, Prahlad Street,
Ansari Road, Darya Ganj,
New Delhi - 110002
Ph. : 23275511, 23257835
e-mail : commonwealthbooks@gmail.com

Typesetting by :

Arnav Computers
Delhi

Printed at :
Roshan Offset Printers
New Delhi

Preface

There is no way to really get to know a culture without knowledge of its slangs and colloquialisms. Although slang and colloquialisms may not be accepted as formal language, they do play a part in how we as humans communicate. The present work is a valuable dictionary of the rich colourful language expressions—slangs and colloquialisms.

Textbook knowledge of a language will only take you so far. Most languages have a large amount of slang utilised by those speaking it. This volume that lists hundreds of common slang words and colloquial expressions. Entries include grammatical information, the definition in English, a sentence or phrase to illustrate usage, and an English translation of the example and, where applicable, a corresponding English slang expression.

This book fills a void in colloquial material available for English speakers and is better than many similar slang dictionaries that can be found for the more widely spoken languages. Because of the nature of slang, this book might contain certain expressions that some readers might find offensive.

Josna Sebastian

A

Abdabs: Terror, the frights, nerves. Often heard as *the screaming abdabs*. Also very occasionally 'habdabs'.

Abysinnia: A jocular and intentional mispronunciation of "I'll be seeing you!"

AC/DC: Bisexual.

Ace: Excellent, wonderful.

Acid: The drug LSD. Lysergic acid diethylamide.

Acid house: The dance music scene that pre-empted 'rave' in Britain, and began the long association of 'house' music and 'ecstasy'.

Ackers: Money. From the Egyptian *akka*.

Action man: A man who participates in macho activities.

Adam and Eve: Believe. Cockney rhyming slang. E.g."I don't Adam and Eve it, it's not true!":

Aerated: Over-excited. Becoming obsolete, although still heard used by older generations. Often mispronounced as *aeriated*.

Afto: Afternoon.

Afty: Afternoon. E.g."Are you going to watch the game this afty?"

Aggro: Aggressive troublemaking, violence, aggression.
Abb. of aggravation.

Agony aunt: A woman who provides answers to readers letters in a publication's agony column.

Air biscuit: An expulsion of air from the anus, a fart.

Air guitar: An imaginary guitar played by rock music fans whilst listening to their favourite tunes.

Airhead: A stupid person.

Airlocked: Drunk, intoxicated.

Airy-fairy: Lacking in strength, insubstantial.

Aks: To ask. E.g."I aksed him to move his car from the driveway."

Alan Whickers: Knickers; underwear. Rhyming slang, often shortened to Alans.

Alcopop: Sweet, ready-mixed fruit drinks containing alcohol.

Aled (up): Drunk, intoxicated by alcohol, usually beer (ale).

Alkie: An alcoholic. Also spelt alky.

All mod cons: All the fixtures and fittings necessary and expected

All time loser:	A public house, a bar. Rhyming slang on 'boozer'.
All to cock:	Messed up, useless, wrong.
All to pot:	Wrong, messed up. E.g."Our whole holiday went all to pot when Dad got arrested for being drunk."
All-nighter:	A club night or event that goes on all night.
Allow (it):	Forget it, don't bother.
Almond rocks:	Socks. Cockney rhyming slang, often shortened to *almonds.*:
Alright:	Hello. A greeting. No answer is expected to what is inherently a question. Northern dialect has created the phonetic corruption *awreet*.
Amber nectar:	Lager.
Anchors:	Brakes. E.g."I slammed the anchors on and hit my head on the steering wheel."
Ankle-biters:	Children, particularly crawling babies.
Anorak:	An often socially inept person, having an obsessive interest in a hobby or subject. Usually has little or no fashion sense, and errs towards eccentricity.
Antwacky:	Old fashioned. Possibly from antique(y).

E.g."Oh no way! I'm not wearing those shoes, they're so antwacky."

Any cop: Of value, of any worth. E.g."Have you heard their new CD? I heard it was rubbish but do you think it's any cop?"

Any road: Adv. Anyway. Also spelt anyroad.

Apeth: A pet name for a silly person. A shortening of daft apeth. Apeth, derived from haypneeworth (half a penny's worth) but pronounced ha'p'orth.

Apple (core): Cockney rhyming slang on 'score'.

Apple core: *Rhyming Slang* for 'score'.

April: Bottom, buttocks, 'arse'. Rhyming slang from April in Paris rhyming with arris.

Arching for it: (like a cat on heat) a term sometimes used to describe a young lady who is sexually fired up.

Argue the toss: Vrb phrs. To argue or dispute loudly and at length.

Argy-bargy: Trouble, noisy quarrelling, arguing.

Arris: Buttocks, 'arse'. Convoluted Cockney rhyming slang for 'arse'; Arris, an abbreviation of Aristotle.

Arrows: the game darts - pron. "arras".

Arrows: Darts, the equipment and the game itself.

Arse: The buttocks. The similar 'ass' isn't used as frequently, remaining more of an Americanism.

Arse about face: Back to front.

Arse about tit: Back to front.

Arse load: In large quantities, a lot of, a great amount. E.g." She's given me arse loads of paperwork to complete before lunch."

Arse over kettle: Fall over. Also arse over tea kettle.

Arse over tip: Fall over, head over heels. E.g."She went arse over tip on the ice outside."

Arse over tit: Meaning the same as 'arse over tip'.

Arse-about-face: something that is in a mess or crooked, e.g. "Look at the state of that shelf you just put up, it's all arse about face!".

Arse-bandit: A homosexual male.:

Arsed: Concerned, bothered. Usually heard in the negative sense of can't be arsed. E.g."I can't be arsed with work today, it's too damned hot."

Arseface: An ugly person.

Arsehat: A contemptible person. Anglicized version of the original U.S. version, 'asshat'.

Arse-hole: An idiot, contemptible person.

Arseholed: very drunk, e.g. "I got totally arseholed on Saturday night.".

Arseholed: Very drunk.

Arse-lick: To grovel, ingratiate oneself.

Arse-licker: A sycophant.

Arse-licking: Sycophantic behaviour.

Arsemonger: A contemptible person. Also arse monger.

Arse-on: A bad mood. E.g."Keep out of Andy's way, he's got a the arse-on."

Arse-up: A shambles, a 'cock-up'.

Arsewipe: Toilet paper.

Arsey: Moody.

Article: An objectionable person. E.g."Come on, go and tidy your bedroom you lazy article."

Arty-farty: Pretentiously artistic.

Arvo: Afternoon.

As fuck: An intensifier. E.g."It was rusty as fuck, so wasn't worth repairing."

As right as rain: Satisfactory, comfortable, well.

Ass bandit: A homosexual male.

Ass clown: An idiot.

Asshat: A contemptible person.

Asswipe: Meaning the same as 'arsewipe'

Aunt Annie: *Rhyming Slang* for 'fanny' (vagina).

Auntie: Affectionate and dated pet name for the BBC (The British Broadcasting Corporation).

Aussie kiss: Cunnilingus, from the fact that it's the same a French Kiss, but given down under.

Aviation blonde: A female with hair dyed blonde. From blonde hair, black box - black box being an aeroplane flight recorder and 'box' also being slang for vagina.

Avvy: Afternoon.

Away and shite: Go away! [North-east use]

Awlarse: A contemptible person. Also auldarse, allarse. Possibly from old arse.

Awright: An alternative spelling and pronunciation of alright (all right).

Axe: A guitar.

Axe wound: Vagina.

Ayrton Senna: *Modern Rhyming Slang* for 'tenner' (ten pound note), e.g. "i've only got an Ayrton left to last me the month!".

Ayrton: Ten pounds (monetary). Rhyming slang for tenner, on Ayrton Senna, the motor racing driver.

Ay-up!: A greeting, hello.

B

Babby:	A baby, child.
Babe:	1. Usually applied to a young attractive female but also said with reference to males.
	2. An affectionate form of address.
Babe magnet	An attractive or sexually desirable male.
Baboon:	An oaf, a fool.
Backdoor:	A euphemism for the anus.
Backhander:	A bribe.
Backie:	A pillion ride on a bycycle.
Back passage:	The rectum.
Back scuttle:	Anal intercourse.
Backy:	Abb. Of tobacco.
	Another variation is Backo.
Bacon sarnie:	Pakistani. Rhyming slang.
Bad:	Good, excellent.
Bad egg:	A miscreant, a corrupt person, an untrustworthy person.

Badger: To bother incessantly. E.g."Stop badgering her, she's not interested in buying another pair of your cheap trainers."

Bad hair day: 1. A day when one is unable to arrange one's hair into a satisfactory and pleasing style.

2. Used figuratively for a problematic and difficult day.

Bad mouth: To insult or denigrate.

Bad news: A troublesome person.

Baffies: Slippers.

Bag: 1. An ugly woman.

2. An objectionable and unpleasant person.

3. Meaning that which interests. E.g."What's your bag ? Mine is dance music."

Bag (of sand): Rhyming slang on a 'grand'. Often shortened to bag.

Baggin(g): A snack or food taken between meals. Heard pronounced as baggin.

Bag lady: A homeless woman who carries her worldly possessions in bags.

Bag of bones: A very thin or emaciated person or animal.

Bag off: To commune with someone sexually desirable, occasionally in so much as having sex. E.g."She bagged off with that"

Bag of shit: A general disparaging term, used for either a person or thing. E.g."He hadn't slept or washed for 4 days and looked like a bag of shite."

Bag of wank: A thing or situation that is not very good, that is poor, without value. E.g."I was expecting a big bag of wank, but I actually enjoyed the film, apart from the scene where the dog died."

Bag of washing: A failed parachute or other material based airfoil, such as a handglider.

Bag on: A bad mood.

Bags: To claim as one's own due to being the first to make such a claim. E.g."Bags I go first."

Bagsy: A variation on 'bags' (verb). Basically meaning bags I.

Bahookie: The backside, the bottom, the buttocks.

Bake: The mouth.

Baked bean: The queen. Rhyming slang.

Baldy notion: An idea, a clue. Usually in the negative sense such as "to not have a baldy notion". Often abbreviated to baldy.

Ball-ache: A troublesome and inconvenient task. Also ballache. E.g."I wish I hadn't sold the car, walking 5

	miles to and from work, everyday, is a real ball-ache."
Ball and chain:	A wife or girlfriend.
Ball-bag:	The scrotum.
Ballocks:	1. The testicles. A variation on 'bollocks'. S.E. from 1200s, slang from mid 1800s.
	2. Rubbish, nonsense.
Balloon knot:	The anus. From its appearance.
Ballsed-up:	Ruined, in a mess.
Balls-up:	A mess up, a 'cock-up'. E.g."I've made a right balls-up of my exams." To make a mess of a situation.
Balm:	A bread bun or roll.
Balmy:	Insane, crazy. A derivative of the earlier 'barmy.'
Baloney:	Nonsense. Also spelt boloney.
Baltic:	Very cold, with respect to the weather or air temperature.
Bam:	A foolish and objectionable person. Abbreviated form of 'bampot'.
Bampot:	A foolish and objectionable person.
Bamstick:	A foolish and objectionable person.
Banana:	A penis.

Barry: Good, nice.

Barry White: 1. Rubbish, nonsense.

2. An act of defecation.

Barse: The perineum. From the area between the balls and the arse.

Bar steward: A pun on 'bastard'.

Base over apex: Head over heels, upside down. E.g."His front wheel hit a rock on the road and he went base over apex."

Bash: 1. An event, a party. E.g."I'm having a bash at a club for my birthday."

2. An attempt. E.g."Try having a bash at the next question if you can't answer the first."

Basket: A euphemism for 'bastard'.

Basket case: An emotionally unstable person, a dysfunctional person, a completely useless person.

Bastard: 1. A contemptible person.

2. A pitiable person. E.g. "That poor bastard never stood a chance once the avalanche started."

Bastarding: An intensifier. E.g."I'm sorry for being late, I missed the bastarding bus again!"

Bathers: Swimming/bathing costume.

Bat in the cave: A globule or lump of nasal mucus when visible up a nostril.

Battered: Very intoxicated by drink or drugs.

Battle cruiser: A pub, bar. From rhyming slang for 'boozer'.

Batty: Crazy, eccentric.

Batty boy: A homosexual male. From batty meaning buttocks. Also battyboy, battyman.

Batty crease: The area between the buttocks.

Batty rider: Skimpy shorts that 'ride' up to expose the wearers bottom ('batty') cheeks, usually female attire.

Baw-bag: 1. The scrotum. From 'ball-bag'. 2 A contemptible person.

Bawheid: 1. A bald head.

2. An idiot, buffoon.

Bazzin': Excellent. E.g."That was a bazzin cricket match."

Beach-bum: A person devoted to spending as much time as available on the beach.

Beak: 1. The mouth.

2. A judge or magistrate.

3. Cocaine.

Beakie: The dirt or bodily secretions that accumulate at the corner of the eyes or between the toes.

Beaked up: High on cocaine. E.g."We had a great night, everyone was well beaked up."

Bananas: Insane, mad, hysterical.

Bang: 1. To copulate. A particularly aggressive term.

2. To put or place, the implication being with nonchalence. E.g."I'll bang those in an envelope and send them off first post in the morning."

Banger: 1. A sausage. The English meal of sausages and mashed potato is traditionally called bangers and mash.

2. A delapidated car.

Banging: Sexual intercourse.

Bang on: Exactly, correct.

Bang to rights: Caught red-handed. Police/ criminal vernacular often heard used jocularly.

Banjax: To ruin.

Banjaxed: 1. Ruined, defeated. Originally Anglo-Irish use, popularized by the UK radio/TV presenter Terry Wogan with his book of the same name.

2. Drunk, by extension of meaning

Banjo: To hit or punch.

Banjo'd: Drunk, intoxicated.

Banjo string: The frenulum of the penis.

Banko: Abb. Of bank holiday (a national holiday).

Baps: Breasts. E.g."Look at the baps on her!"

Bar: One pound sterling.

Barbie: Abb. Of barbecue.

Barbs: Abb. Of barbituates.

Barcode: A supporter of the Newcastle United football club. From their team kit being designed around black and white vertical stripes, like a barcode.

Bare: A lot of, significant amount. E.g."It's just bare hype, the film's just famous faces and no plot."

Barf: To vomit, probably onomatapoeic in origin. E.g."He's feeling woozy, I think he's gonna barf his dinner up."

Barking: Insane, crazy. Short for barking mad.

Barking spider: The anus.

Barmcake: 1. A lighthearted term for a fool or idiot.

2. A bread bun. Also barm cake.

Barmpot: A silly person. A lighted-hearted expression.

Barnet: Hair. From the Cockney rhyming slang barnet fair.

Barney: An argument.

Barney (rubble): Trouble. Rhyming slang.

Bean: An ecstasy pill.

Beanfeast: A party, celebratory event.

Bean-flicker: A lesbian. The bean refers to the clitoris.

Beano: A party. Abbreviated form of 'beanfeast'.

Bear: A large hairy man.

Beard: 1. A woman who is seen to be romantically linked with a gay man, so protecting his true sexuality from public scrutiny - often associated with celebrities.

2. Of a woman, pubic hair.

Bearded clam: The female genitals, inclusive of pubic hair.

Beat the bishop: To masturbate.

Beat the meat: To masturbate. E.g."My son seems to be preoccupied with beating his meat at every possible hour of the day."

Beaver: The female genitals, implying the inclusion of pubic hair.

Beaver cleaver: Penis.

Beaver leaver: A homosexual male. Due to not being interested in 'beaver' and leaving it alone.

Beddable: Sexually desirable, from being good enough to take to bed.

Bedfordshire: Bed or bedtime.

Bed hair: Dishevelled hair, as may result from a good night's sleep.

Bedsit: Abb. Of bed-sitter or bed-sitting room. A small apartment whereby the bedroom also serves as a sitting room (living room).

Beeb: 1. The commonly used nickname for the BBC (British Broadcasting Corporation), the nationally owned television production and broadcasting company.

2. Nickname for the BBC Micro computer, an early form of home computer from the 1980s.

Beef: 1. Muscly, strong looking males. 2. A complaint, a grievance, problems (with something). E.g."If you've got a beef about the decision, then fill in the appropriate appeal forms."

Beef curtains: The female genitals.

Beer baby: A protruding belly, from drinking excessive amounts of beer, that makes its owner look pregnant.

Beer belly: A bulging stomach caused by drinking large quantities of beer.

Beemer: A BMW automobile.

Beer goggles: The impaired judgement from the excessive consumption of alcohol (beer) that makes an otherwise unappealing person or thing seem attractive.

Beer o'clock: The time one feels is most appropriate for some alcoholic refreshment , such as beer. Often used specifically to mean the end of the working day.

Beer scooter: The supposed transport one must have taken to get home when very drunk and as there is no recollection of how one did get home.

Beer tits: Fatty deposits on the breasts of a male, arising through excessive beer drinking.

Bees and honey: Money. Rhyming slang.

Bee's knees: The best. This term originates from the prolific slang of the Flappers along with the similar 'cats whiskers'.

Bee stings: Small breasts.

Beetle: To hurry. E.g."I've just spent 2 hours beetling around the shopping precinct looking for a gift for Mick."

Beetle bonnet: The female mons pubis, from its vague resemblence to the bonnet of a Volkswagen Beetle car.

Beggar: Euphemism for 'bugger'.

Begging for it: A general comment on a person's supposed, if not actual, yearning for sexual intimacies. E.g. "Cor, look at her! She's begging for it."

Bejesus!:	An Anglo-Irish corruption of the exclamation by Jesus! Expressing surprise or annoyance.
Bell:	To telephone (someone). E.g."I'll bell you tonight with the news."
Bell end:	1. The head of the penis, being vaguely bell shaped. Also bellend.
	2. A contemptible person, an idiot.
Belly-ache:	A complaint. To complain persistently.
Belly timber:	Food.
Belly-up:	1. Dead.
	2. Failed, bankrupt.
Belt:	To hit.
	1. A hit. E.g."If you don't shut up moaning i'll give you a belt 'round the head."
	2. A drink, by extension of meaning 1. E.g."Have a belt of that brandy, it'll warm you up."
Belter:	An excellent thing or event.
Belting:	Outstanding, wonderful.
Bender:	1. An excessive bout of drinking, but more recently also inclusive of a drug taking spree.
	2. A homosexual. Possibly derived from gender bender, or from being the passive partner, bending over to receive sex, as opposed to being the thruster.

Benny: 1. A tantrum, a fit of anger.

2. A person from the Falkland Islands.

Bent: 1. Homosexual, as opposed to 'straight'.

2. Criminal, corrupt. E.g."You can usually buy your freedom; the cops are bent and paid poorly."

Berk: An idiot, objectionable person. Derived from the rhyming slang Berkshire Hunt or Berkeley Hunt, meaning 'cunt'.

Better half: One's wife, husband or partner.

Betty Swollox: Perspiring, uncomfortable or itchy testicles. A spoonerism and literally *sweaty bollocks.*

Bevvied up: Drunk. Occasionally shortened to *bevvied.*

Bevvy: A general term for an alcoholic drink. Taken from the word *beverage.*

Bezzy mates: Best friends. E.g."They've been bezzy mates since they were at nursery together."

Biatch: A contemptible person, usually woman. Alternative form of 'bitch'.

Bible basher: A fanatical preacher of religion.

Bible thumper: Meaning the same as 'bible basher'.

Bicky: A biscuit.

Biddy: A woman, usually referring to an elderly woman and often reinforced with the word *old*.

Biff: To hit. E.g."He biffed his head on the low ceiling." The vagina.

Biffa: An ugly person, often assumed to be overweight, but also heard as *fat biffa*.

Biffin's bridge: The perineum; the area between the anus and the vulva, or scrotum.

Biffon: The perineum. The place where the man's testicles would hit during vigorous sexual intercourse.

Biftah: 1. A cigarette.

2. A marijuana or cannabis cigarette.

Big cheese: A very important person.

Big style: Greatly. E.g."Yeah she's into him big-style."

Big time: The upper levels of power, success. E.g."She's hit the big time with getting that fifty thousand pound contract."

Big up: To praise, to acclaim. Also to *big oneself up* or to *big it up*.

Bike: A promiscuous woman, often with respect to the immediate district or locality.

Bilge (water): Nonsense, rubbish. E.g."You are talking absolute bilge!"

Bills: Underwear. Rhyming slang on Bill Grundy's, meaning undies.

Billy Amphetamine Sulphate. Abb. Of 'Billy Whizz', a cartoon character from the children's magazine Beano; Billy Whizz does everything with exceptional speed and energy.

Billy goat: A coat. Rhyming slang.

Billy no mates: A person who appears to have no friends.

Billy-o: A lot, greatly, quickly etc. E.g"She's been moaning like billy-o all morning, wanting me to hang out the washing, clean the car, do the hoovering, mow the lawn, i've had enough."

Billy willy: A shrivelled penis, from imbibing amphetamine sulphate or other drugs that cause such a physiological reaction.

Bimble: An ambling walk. E.g."I'm just going for a bimble to the shops, back in 20 minutes." To wander aimlessly, to amble.

Bimbo: A young attractive, empty headed woman.

Bimmer: A BMW car.

Bin: To throw away, to discard.

Bin-bag: To terminate a relationship. From the returning of possessions in a big bag, a disposable bag made of black polythene.

Binge: A spree, often involving food or alcohol. To go on a spree.

Bingo wings: Fatty, folds of flesh on the underarms of overweight women, who might commonly be seen at Bingo nights.

Bin lid: An adolescent. Rhyming slang for kid.

Binnie: A refuse collector. A variation on 'binman'.

Binman: A refuse collector, a dustbin man.

Bin off: 1. To discard, throw away. 2. To terminate a relationship.

Bins: Spectacles.

Bint: A woman. From the Arabic 'bint' meaning girl or daughter.

Bird: 1. A female. Use can be taken as offensive. E.g."Did you see that bird at the back of the bus!"

2. A girlfiend, when used in conjunction with a possessive pronoun, such as my bird.

Birdbrained: Stupid, lacking commonsense.

Biscuit arsed: Dirty, filthy. Also biscuit ersed, from Scottish pronunciation.

Bit: A woman. Abb. Of 'bit of fluff' or 'bit of skirt', generally a person viewed sexually.

Bitch: 1. A contemptible woman. Used on the gay scene to describe an equally despised male.

2. A woman. Derog/Offens.

Bitch piss: Sweet, ready-mixed fruit and alcohol drink.

Bitch tits: 1. Overly developed fatty deposits on the male breasts, the medical condition of gynecomastia.

2. As the above, having fatty breast tissue, but due to excessive drinking of beer.

Bit of all right: Something excellent. Often heard used with reference to a sexually attractive person. E.g."She's a bit of alright! I'm going to ask her for a date."

Bit of fluff: A sexual partner.

Bit of rough: A sexual partner below one's normal standards or believed class.

Bit of skirt: A woman or women. A male expression for females viewed sexually. Also abbreviated to 'skirt'.

Bit of spare: A sexually available person.

Bit of stuff: A sexually desirable person or persons.

Bit on the side: 1. A sexual relationship extra to one's usual partner, an affair.

2. The other person in a sexual affair.

Bits: A euphemism for the genitals, male or female.

Bits and bats: Miscellaneous items.

Bits and bobs Miscellaneous items.

Biz: Rubbish, nonsense. E.g."Don't go and see that new amateur play at the theatre, it was biz."

Bizzies: The police. Possibly derived from the expression busy body.

BJ: Oral sex.

Blabbermouth: A person who reveals too much in conversation, a gossip.

Bladdered: Drunk.

Blag: To lie, or use clever talk with profit as an objective, to wheedle or persuade for gain. E.g."I blagged a lift to work with my sister but had to get the bus home."

Blag artist: A person with a reputation for using clever talk for self gain.

Blagger: A robber, especially of banks, and often with the use of a weapon or violence.

Blank: To rudely ignore. E.g."Despite being introduced 5 minutes earlier, he just blanked me and continued talking.."

Blaps: Diarrhoea, the illness.

Blart: To cry.

Blast: 1. An inhalation of a cigarette or 'joint'. E.g."Give us a blast on your cigarette, i've just run out."

2. An enjoyable experience. E.g."Wasn't the party last night a blast?"

Blates: Blatantly, blatant.

Blatts: Diarrhoea, the illness. E.g."I daren't leave the house, i've got the blatts."

Blaze: To set alight. Usually with respect to the lighting of cigarettes and marijuana cigarettes, 'joints'.

Blazed: Very intoxicated, or high, on marijuana or cannabis.

Blazin': Smoking marijuana or cannabis.

Bleeder: A person, more often than not one who is objectionable.

Bleeding: Used as an intensive. E.g."That bleeding idiot from next door is drunk again."

Bletch: Mechanical lubricating oil.

Blighter: An insignificant or objectionable person. E.g."This blighter approaches me and asks for a cigarette; sure I say, and then he has the gall to put it in his pocket and says he'll smoke that later and then asks for another to have now."

Blighty: Affectionate name for England as one's home, often used jocularly. Orig. Used by colonial Indian Army, from the Hindustani bilyati, meaning foreign.

Blim: A red hot fragment of cannabis that occasionally fall from lit cannabis cigarettes.

Blim burn: A scorch mark or hole in fabrics and clothing, created by a burning crumb of cannabis.

Blimey!: An exclamation of surprise. An abbreviated form of blind me.

Blimp: A red hot fragment of cannabis that will occasionally fall from alight 'joints', causing small burns to skin, clothing and furnishings. E.g."You could tell he was a heavy smoker, cos he had little holes all over his t-shirt from blimps."

Blinder: An excellent achievement. E.g."Tim's played another blinder."

Blinding: Excellent, wonderful. E.g."We had a blinding time last night."

Blindo: Extremely drunk. From blind drunk.

Bling: Abb. Form of 'bling bling'.

Bling bling: Jewellery.

Bling up: To make showy and visually ostentatious. E.g."I blinged up my car so that I'd get some female attention."

Blinking: Used as an intensifier, but a particularly mild expression. E.g."Your blinkin' washing machine has broken down again." Or "It's blinkin' heavy, this washing machine".

Blinkin' heck: An old fashioned inoffensive exclamation of surprise, often expressed without the 'h'. Also 'heck' can be replaced with 'hell'.

Blithering: 1. An intensifier such as 'bloody'. E.g."How can I have toast when that blithering idiot has just eaten all the bread!"

2. Senseless and excessive talking.

Blither on: To talk incessently and boringly. Blither is a varient spelling of the s.e.blather. E.g."Please stop blithering on, your voice is driving my crazy."

Blitzed: Very intoxicated, drunk.

Bloater: A fat and unnattractive person.

Blob: To bleed through menstruation. E.g."She was blobbing and still wanted sex, but I'm not keen on blood."

Blob strop: Of females, a fit of anger brought on through premenstrual tension.

Blog on: A bad mood.

Bloke: A man.

Blonde moment: A moment of stupidity. Based on the misguided belief that blondes are considerably less intelligent than those with other hair colours.

Blood: A friendly term of address. Orig. Black use for addressing a fellow Black.

Bloodsports: Sexual acts with a woman during the period of her menstruation.

Bloody: Expressing annoyance as an intensifier. E.g."That bloody idiot needs a good thumping."

Bloody hell: An exclamation of surprise or frustration.

Bloody-Nora: An exclamation of surprise or anger.

Bloomer: A mistake.

Blooming: An intensifier. E.g."It's blooming cold outside!"

Blooter: To kick a ball forcefully, often implying without good control.

Blootered: Drunk.

Blotto: Very drunk.

Blow: Cannabis or marijuana. It's interesting to note that in the U.S. it refers to cocaine.

Blow away: 1. To kill.

2. To amaze.

Blowback: A method of sharing a 'joint' between two people, with one person blowing and the other inhaling.

Blow chunks: To vomit. E.g."" Suzanne's been blowing chunks all night so I don't expect her to want any breakfast."

Blower: The telephone. From the 'speaking tube', down which one blew to attract a person's attention prior to having a conversation through it.

Blow it!: A dismissive exclamation of frustration and anger.

Blow job: Fellatio or cunnilingus.

Blow it!: An exclamation of anger or frustration.

Blow its tits off: To be very windy or blustery. E.g."It's still blowing its tits off this morning so we wont be able to go sailing into the bay."

Blow-off: To break wind, but not belching. E.g."As boys seem to spend all night blowing off, I recommend you avoid cleaning their dorm until later in the morning."

Blow one's top: To explode with fury.

Blow one's wad: To ejaculate semen. E.g."It was disgusting, he blew his wad all over my breasts."

Blow out: An excessive spree of drinking, eating, spending or sex.

Blow the gaff To reveal a plot or secret.

Blub: To sob. Possibly onomatopoeic.

Blud: A form of address. Alternative spelling of 'blood'.

Blue rinser: An elderly lady, a lady pensioner. From the habit of some of this particular age group having their hair died with a hint of blue.

Blunt: A marijuana/cannabis cigarette. More specifically, especially in the U.S., a blunt is marijuana rolled in the outer leaves of a cigar.

Blunted: Intoxicated by marijuana. From the term 'blunt'.

Blurt: The vagina.

Boaby: Penis.

Boak: To vomit.

Boat: Face. From the rhyming slang boat race.

Bob: To visit briefly. E.g."I'm just gonna bob down to the corner shop for some fags, do you want anything?"

Bobbins: Rubbish, nonsense, useless.

Bobbinsed: Drunk, intoxicated.

Bobby: A policeman/woman. The name derives from the pet form of the Christian name of Sir Robert Peel, who established the present British police organisation.

Bobby-dazzler: A amazing thing or person.

Bobfoc: A facially unattractive female, who possesses a sexually desirable body. From body off Baywatch, face off Crimewatch; both TV programmes.

Bob (Hope): Marijuana or cannabis. Rhyming slang for 'dope'.

Bo-boes: Sleep. Generally a children's expression.

Bod: A person.

Bodge: 1. To do a poor job or repair.

2. To cobble (something together). E.g."I bodged together that furniture out of driftwood and old egg boxes."

Bodge job: A job done poorly, something cobbled together, a makeshift repair.

Bof: A contemptible, old person. Acronym of boring old fart.

Boff: 1. To break wind, 'fart'.

2. To have sex (with).

Boffin: 1. A person involved in scientific/technical research, usually associated with the wearing of white laboratory coats, glasses, and carrying a clipboard.

2. An intellectual.

Bog: A toilet.

Bog all: Nothing, or a total lack of. E.g."We've bog all chance of winning without our captain and best player."

Bogart: To selfishly hold on to (something). Jocular usage, heard amongst smokers of cannabis/marijuana. E.g."Come on Tim, don't bogart that joint, we all want to get stoned sometime tonight."

Bogey: A tiny ball of nasal mucus.

Bog-eyed: Bleary or tired looking eyed, either from too little sleep or intoxication by drink or drugs.

Boggin: Unpleasant, vile, ugly.

Bog off (!): To go away.

Go away! Leave me alone!

Bog-roll: Toilet paper.

Bog-standard: Normal, average, usual. E.g."It was just a bog-standard Christmas, too much food, too much booze and not enough sleep."

Bogtrotter: An Irish person. Derog/offens.

Boiler: An unattractive woman. Often phrased as old boiler for added derogatory emphasis.

Boke: To vomit.

Bollix: Alternative spelling of 'bollocks'.

Bollock: To reprimand. E.g."My dad bollocked me for stealing money from his wallet! I was only borrowing it."

Bollockbag: The scrotum and testicles.

Bollock-brain: Idiot, imbecile.

Bollocking: A severe reprimand.

Bollocksed: 1. Worn out, ruined, tired.

2. Very intoxicated.

Bollox: Alternative spelling of 'bollocks'.

Bolshie: Angrily provocative. Originating from the socialist revolutionaries the Bolsheviks.

Bomb: 1. Another name for burning cannabis fragments. Variations include bombies and bombers.

2. A small quantity of illicit drugs wrapped in a handrolling cigarette paper, forming a pill like ball.

Bombed out: Incapacitated by drink or drugs. Also shortened to 'bombed'.

Bommie night: Bonfire night. Possibly spelt bombie night from the use of fireworks.

Bonce: The head.

Bone: To have sexual intercourse. The act of having sexual intercourse.

Bonehead: 1. A stupid person.

2. Of a person, having a shaved head.

Boner: An erect penis.

Bone up: To study hard. E.g."I've been boning up on my highway code - my driving exam is next week."

Bong A water pipe used for smoking cannabis or marijuana.

Bongo mag: A pornographic magazine. Abbreviated form of the less commonly heard bongo magazine.

Bonk: To fornicate. An inoffensive expression, generally used more by adolescents.

A sexual act.

Bonkers: 1. Crazy, insane. E.g."He must be bonkers! Imagine going out and getting drunk before meeting his girlfriend's parents for the first time."

2. Eager for, crazy for.

Bonnie: A bonfire.

Bonnie night: Bonfire Night. An annual celebration of the foiling of an attempt to blow up The Houses of Parliament in 1605.

Boob: 1. A mistake.

2. A breast.

Boobicles: Women's breasts. Affectionate usage, often implying small breasts.

Booboo: A mistake. E.g."Oh no! I've just made a classic booboo".

Boob tube: 1. The television.

2. A tight, strapless top worn by females that is a basic tube of material.

Boogie: A dance, usually to pop music.

To dance.

Book: Cool, excellent. Teen and adolescence vernacular, derived from the first choice of words offered on a mobile phone (cellphone) when texting the word cool with predictive text .

Boonies: Rural areas, the countryside. Abb. Of boondocks.

Boot: 1. An unattractive person.

2. As the boot, meaning the 'sack', termination of employment.

Bootneck: A Royal Marine.

Booty: The buttocks. Mainly black use.

Booty call: A call to arrange a sexual rendezvous. Mainly black use.

Booze: Alcoholic drink.

Booze cruise:	A boat trip (usually just one day) to mainland Europe, in order to purchase the considerably cheaper alcohol (and cigarettes) than is available in Britain.
Boozer:	1. A public house, a bar. 2. A person who enjoys regularly drinking alcohol. 3. An alcoholic.
Booze-up:	A drinking spree.
Boracic:	Poor, having no money. Rhyming slang for 'skint', from boracic lint, an ointment, pronounced borrassic.
Bore rigid:	To utterly bore. E.g."He bores me rigid with his tales of wealth, fame, and his sexual conquests."
Bore shitless:	Bore completely. E.g."I was bored shitless by her talking non-stop about her family."
Bore stiff:	Bore completely.
Bosh:	Nonsense, rubbish.
Boss:	Excellent, good.
Boss-eyed:	Cross-eyed or having a squint.
Bossyboots:	A person who bosses others around, a domineering person.
Bost:	Broken. Probably from bust.
Bostin:	Great, good, enjoyable. E.g."She had a bostin figure."

Botch job: 1. A makeshift construction or repair.
2. A thing done badly.

Botch (up): 1. To build or repair in a makeshift manner.
2. To do something badly.

Bottle: Courage, confidence. E.g."Johnny's scared, he's lost his bottle."
To smash a bottle into a person's face, very often a beer bottle after a drinking spree.

Bottle it: 1. To lose courage. Also bottle out.
2. Shut up! Usually imper.

Bottle of chips: An unlikely thing. Used in expressions to add emphasis, such as in 'bent as a bottle of chips', 'queer as a bottle of chips', 'mad as a bottle of chips' etc

Bottler: A person who easily gives up, or loses the courage to complete a task.

Bottom burp: Wind from the anus, a 'fart'. Also abbreviated to botty burp.

Bottom feeder: A despicable person.

Bottomless pit: A person with an insatiable appetite for food.

Botty: The buttocks. Also abbreviated to bot. Children's expression.

Boulder houlder: A brassiere. Jocular male usage.

Bouncer: A person employed to eject troublemakers from clubs or events. These days they prefer the title of security.

Bovver: Trouble. A corruption of bother, derived from cockney pronounciation.

Bovverboots: Sturdy heavy boots.

Bowfin: Disgusting, unpleasant.

Box: 1. Anus.

2. Vagina.

Box clever: To act shrewdly or in a manner so as to outwit someone.

Boxed: Intoxicated by drugs.

Boy dem: A police officer. Also boydem.

Boy racer: A young man who has a penchant for fast cars and reckless driving.

Boysie: Affectionate term of address, usually for a younger male.

Bozo: An objectionable person, an idiot.

Brace and bit: An act of defecation. Rhyming slang on 'shit'.

Brad pitt: 1. An act of defecation. Rhyming slang on 'shit'.

2. When plural, as *Brad Pitts,* meaning a bout of diarrhoea. Rhyming slang on 'shits'.

Brain: To hit on the head. E.g."If you don't tidy your room now, i'll brain you."

Brained: Extreme drug intoxication, affecting the mental faculties.

Brain fart: An inability to think clearly, or a moment of forgetfulness.

Brammer: A person or thing that is outstanding. Also brahma.

Bran new: Excellent, respectable.

Brass: 1. Money.

2. Prostitute. Short for *brass nail,* rhyming slang for tail, which is itself slang for, amongst other things, a woman and prostitute.

Brassed off: Fed-up, annoyed. E.g."I'm brassed off all this bad weather."

Brass monkeys: Of the weather or air temperature, very cold. E.g."Wear a hat and scarf, it's brass monkeys out there."

Brass-neck: Impudence, cheek, nerve. Also brass-necked.

Brassy: Very cold. From the phrase, 'cold enough to freeze the balls off a brass monkey'.

Brast: To burst.

Bray: To beat up, thrash.

Bread: Money.

Breakbeat: 1. A style of drum patterns originating from jazz.

2. A dance music genre epitomised by speedy 'samples' of

breakbeats. Originally 'rave' specific but developed into 'jungle' and 'drum and bass.'

Bredrin: Friend, brother. From the archaic s.e. Brethren.

Breeder: A heterosexual. From the fact that heterosexuals actively procreate, or breed.

Brekky: Abb. Of breakfast. Also the variant, brekkers.

Brer: A term of address, for a friend. From brother.

Brew: 1. A cup of tea, or more generally a warm drink.

2. Alcoholic drink, usually beer or lager.

Brewers droop: An inability to achieve or maintain a penile erection due to excessive consumption of alcohol.

Brew-up: To make a cup or pot of tea.

Brick: A helpful and reliable person.

Brickie: Abb. Of bricklayer.

Brick-it: To be very scared, terrified.

Brick shithouse: Something strong and very sturdy. Usually in the phrase 'built like a brick shithouse'.

Brief: A solicitor or barrister.

Brill: Excellent, superb. An abbreviation of brilliant. E.g."We had a brill night, dancing for 8 hours."

Brilliant: Excellent, marvellous.

Bring off: To help achieve orgasm.

Bristols: Breasts. From the rhyming slang Bristol City - titty.

Britneys: Beers. Rhyming slang on Britney Spears. Very popular and recent expression.

Bro: Abb. Of brother.:

Brolly: An umbrella.

Broo: Unemployment bureau or benefits office. An abbreviated form of bureau. E.g."I was laid off work yesterday, so I'm going down the broo to sign on for social security."

Brooky: An abbreviated name frequently used for the British TV soap Brookside, which ceased transmission in 2003.

Brown bread: Dead. Cockney rhyming slang.

Browned off: Upset, fed up, miserable.

Browneye: The anus.:

Brown hatter: A homosexual male.

Brownie point: A hypothetical award for achievement, usually given as a backhanded compliment for sycophantic behaviour.

Brown-nose: To overly praise or behave sycophantically, i.e. To 'arse-lick'. E.g."Tom's in the manager's office brown-nosing - hoping to get that promotion."

Brown-noser: A sycophant.

Browns: Cigarette(s). E.g."Will you pass me a browns, I'm gasping for a smoke."

Brown trout: A lump of excrement.

Bruce Lees: Erect and prominent nipples. A play on words, from Bruce Lee (the actor famous for his Martial Arts skills/films) being a hard Nip (a tough and unyielding person from Japan, or rather oriental, being as Bruce Lee was American born and whose parents were from Hong Kong).

Brum: The City of Birmingham. From the word brummagem.

Brummie: A native of Birmingham.

Bruv: A term of address, usually for a friend. A corruption of brother.

Bubbies: Female breasts.

Bubble: To inform. From the rhyming slang bubble and squeak meaning speak. E.g."If you bubble me to the boss, i'll lose my job."

Bubble (bath): A laugh. Rhyming slang. E.g."You're having a bubble James, if you think I'm going to give you twenty notes."

Bubble butt:	A well rounded, sexually attractive bottom. Also bubblebutt.
Bubbled:	Found out, discovered. E.g."I can't get any more of those cheap Reebok trainers, I was bubbled hiding ten pairs in my car so lost my job."
Bubblehead:	An empty headed and stupid person.
Bucket down:	To rain heavily. The past tense is bucketing down.
Bucket fanny:	A large, expansive vagina. Often used in a context that implies promiscuity.
Buck naked:	Totally naked.
Buckshee:	Free, without charge.
Buck up	To make happy or more cheerful.
Bucky:	Abb. Form of Buckfast wine.
Bud:	Marijuana, or occasionally cannabis. Specifically the part of the marijuana plant that is smoked.
Budge up:	To move, in order to make room for someone. E.g."Budge up and let Bob sit down."
Buff:	Good looking, attractive.
Buftie:	A homosexual male. Also bufty.
Bug	1. To annoy, to bother.
	2. To spy on via a concealed microphone.

Bug-eyed: Having large bulbous eyes.

Bugger: 1. An objectionable person.

2. A person. Also used in a sense of pity.

3. A situation or event that is difficult or distressing. E.g."It's a real bugger Pete catching the flu on his summer holidays."

Bugger-all: Absolutely nothing at all. E.g."There's bugger-all we can do about it now, the police are here and we're trapped."

Buggeration!: An exclamation of annoyance or surprise.

Buggered: Worn out, broken, ruined.

Buggergrips: Sideburns, facial hair on the side of a man's face.

Bugger it!: Exclamation of frustration.

Buggerlugs: A term of address, usually affectionate use.

Bugger me!: An exclamation of surprise.

Bugger-off: Get lost, clear off. Usually said in annoyance and in the imper.

Bugger-up: To mess up, to get wrong. E.g."It's no good, we may aswell go home, he's buggered up the evening by getting drunk."

Buggery: Used as an intensifier in denials such as 'did I buggery!' or 'like buggery she did'.

Bugger you: An exclamation of annoyance.

Bugle: Cocaine.

Builder's bum: Describing the top of the buttocks being in sight above the waistline of trousers when kneeling or bending. Stereotypical image of builders.

Bulge: A euphemism for the male genitals usually from being apparent through clothing.

Bull: Nonsense. A modification of 'bullshit'.

To polish, clean.

Bull dyke: A masculine lesbian. Typifies the heterosexual necessity to impart male traits in a derogatory fashion, however the term is used and accepted within the scene.

Bullshit: Nonsense, rubbish, egocentric boasting.

To lie, fib.

Bullshitter: An egocentric boaster, a teller of untruths.

Bum: 1. The buttocks or anus.

2. A objectionable person.

3. A beggar, homeless person.

Bum around: To mess about, to laze about.

Bumbaclot: An idiot, an objectionable person. Also occasionally spelt bumbaclat or bumbaclut.

Bum-bag:	A small pouch worn around the waist or hips, held in place by a strap or belt, and used to hold valuables and money. The U.S. equivalent is a fanny pack.
Bum bandit:	A homosexual male.
Bum-boy:	A homosexual male.
Bum-chum:	A person with an apparently overly close friendship with another person. Although the underlying implication is of homosexuality, the expression is mainly used by children, with little true awareness of the sexual slur they may be imbuing.
Bum cleavage:	The area between the buttocks.
Bumf:	Printed documents and papers that are of little interest or importance. Abb. Of 'bum fodder'.
Bumfluff:	Adolescent facial hair growth.
Bum fodder:	1. Printed papers and documents that are of no interest, and are viewed as only being suitable for using as toilet paper. 2. Toilet paper.
Bum-freezer:	A short jacket, that doesn't cover one's bottom (bum), and thus leaves it vulnerable to the cold.
Bummer:	A bad time, a bad experience, a disappointment.

Bum nugget: 1. Small faecal remnants that have stuck to one's anal hairs.
2. An idiot, contemptible person.

Bum-numbing: Of work, a task, or event, exceedingly tiring or tedious. Also bum-numbingly.

Bumph: Papers or documents, usually of little interest or importance. Short for 'bum fodder'.

Bump off: To murder.

Bump start: To help motivate, assist in promoting action. E.g."I think we need to bump start the project with an ideas session."

Bump tummies: To have sexual intercourse.

Bump uglies: To have sexual intercourse. E.g."My mum knows we're bumping uglies but she doesn't mind as long as we are careful."

Bum steer: An imparting of false information.

Bumtag: A faecal deposit that has adhered to the anal hairs of a person or animal.

Bumwad: Toilet paper.

Bun: A smoke, particularly marijuana. From burn.

Bunce: Money.

Bundle: A large quantity of money.

Bung: To give or throw. E.g."Go on, bung her an extra tenner for trying."

Bungalow: An idiot. From not having much up upstairs.

Bunk off: To shirk one's duties. A common adolescent's term for avoiding school lessons.

Bunk up. Sexual intercourse. E.g."I thought if I brought her drinks all night I'd at least get a bunk up."

Bunning: Smoking marijuana or cannabis.

Bunny boiler: An obsessive and psychotic woman. Taken from a scene in the film Fatal Attraction.

Bunny hugger: An animal lover.

Buppie: Bread and butter. Usually a children's expression.

Burn rubber: To depart quickly. Derived from burning tyre rubber from excessive acceleration with a motor vehicle.

Burp the worm: To masturbate, of males.

Bursting: Desperately needing to urinate.

Bush: 1. The female genitals, but alluding to the pubic hair.

2. Marijuana.

Bust: A police raid on a person and/or property.

Bustin: Eager. Probably a corruption of *bursting*. E.g."I'm bustin for a pint and a smoke."

Bust one's guts: To work with great effort.

Butch: 1. Tough looking, masculine.
2. A masculine lesbian.

Butchers: A look. From the Cockney rhyming slang *butcher's hook*. E.g."Let's have a butchers at it before you put it back."

Butt: The buttocks. S.e from 1400s until 1600s.

Butters: 1. Ugly.
2. Rubbish, useless, of no value.

Butt fucker: A homosexual male.

Butt munch: A contemptible or objectionable person.

Butt muncher: A homosexual male.

Butt naked: Naked.

Butt out: An impolite request to keep one's nose out of something. E.g."Butt out John, it's none of your business."

Butt pirate: A homosexual male.

Butt plug: A plug, usually made of rubber, for insertion in the anus during sex.

Butt ugly: Very ugly.

Butty: 1. A sandwich. The term originates in the North of England but has gained national use. Also spelt *buttie*.

2. Term of address for a friend.

Buzz: 1. A telephone call. E.g. "i'll give you a buzz with the details in the morning."

2. A thrill. E.g. "She gets a buzz from being provocative and causing arguments."

Buzz along: A cheery request to hurry off.

Buzz-cut: A short haircut using electric clippers.

Buzzin': Thrilled and full of energy, often as a result of partaking in illicit drugs.

Buzz off: To go away, to leave.

Go away:

By gum: An exclamation of surprise or amazement.

By (h)eck: An exclamation of surprise. Dialectically the *h* is dropped.

C

Cabbage: 1. A person in a catatonic state or seemingly brain dead.

2. The female genitals.

Cack: 1. Rubbish, nonsense.

2. Excrement.

Cacker: 1. Gypsy, traveller.

2. General derogatory term for any number of people with various social or behavioural problems, such as petty criminals, troublemakers, 'chavs'.

Cack-handed: Clumsy, without manual dexterity.

Cackhander: A left handed person.

Cacky: Dirty, rubbishy.

Caff: A cafe.

Cake-hole: The mouth. E.g."Shut your cake-hole and get on with your work."

Call (someone): To insult (someone).

Camel's hoof: An impression of the female genitals/vulva as seen through tightly worn clothing.

Camel toe: An impression of the female genitals/vulva as seen through tightly worn clothing. Also camel's toe and camel toes.

Camp: An effeminate style and mannerism affected mainly by 'gays', however anyone can 'camp it up.'

Camp it up: To overact in an affected manner. E.g."If you want to see people camping it up, walk down Canal Street in the Gay Village in Manchester on a Saturday night."

Cancer stick: A cigarette.

Caned: Intoxicated.

Caner: A person who indulges in excessive bouts of drug or alcohol use.

Cane: To hurt, to pain. E.g."It caned severely when I tried to walk on it, and I knew it was broken."

Cane (it) 1. To travel at great speed. E.g."I caned it down the motorway and got there in record time."

2. To overindulge in drugs or alcohol. E.g."I've been caning whizz (amphetamine sulphate) all weekend and had no sleep for 3 days."

Cank: To talk, chat or gossip.

Cankles: Usually of women, fat ankles that lack definition and seem to merge with the calves of the leg. A combination of the words ankle and calf. Also occasionally 'kankles'.

Canny: Good, nice, pleasant. E.g."She was a canny lass."

Cans: Headphones.:

Cant: 1. To talk, to speak.

2. To tell tales, to lie.:

Can't be arsed: Can't be bothered.

Cardie: A cardigan.

Cark (it): To die. Also 'kark it'. E.g."Princess Diana carked it in car crash in Paris."

Carpet muncher: 1. A lesbian.

2. A person who performs cunnilingus.

Carrot cruncher: A person from the country, a rural dweller.

Carrot top: Nickname for a person with red/ginger hair.

Carry out: Alcohol brought from a bar with the intention of taking it home or away.

Carry the can: Vrb phrs. To take responsibility for a mistake. E.g."I'm not carrying the can for your inability to control your kids."

Casey: A leather football.

Catch flies: To look blankly with one's mouth open.

Catch some z's: Get some sleep. Pronounced catch some zeds. Original U.S. version is pronounced catch some Zees

Catch you later!: Goodbye!

Cat's pyjamas: The best.

Cat's whiskers: The best, most sublime thing or person.

Cattle truck: 1. To have sexual intercourse.

2. To ruin, destroy.

Cattled: Broken, worn out. From the rhyming slang 'cattle truck' and hence meaning 'fucked'. E.g."Looks like we are staying at home for the weekend, the car's cattled."

Cavalier: An uncircumcised penis and consequently a male with such.

Chalfonts: Haemorrhoids. Rhyming slang. From Chalfont St Giles, a town in Buckinghamshire, rhyming with piles

Chalk (farm): Arm. Rhyming slang.:

Champion: Excellent. Also used as an exclamation.

Champs: Abb. Of champagne.

Chang: Cocaine.

Channel surfing: Switching from one television channel to another in search of an interesting programme.

Chap: 1. A man. E.g."This chap came up to me and told me to shut my mouth."

2. A form of address. Usually associated with the speech of the upper classes. E.g."I say old chap, fancy joining us for a gin and tonic?"

Chapel hat pegs: Erect and prominent female nipples.

Char: Tea. From the Chinese cha.

Charged: High on drugs.

Charity-case: A person deemed rightly or wrongly to be in need of charity, whether poor or handicapped in some manner.

Charlie: 1. Cocaine. Probably the most commonly used slang term for this drug.

2. A fool, an idiot.

Charlies Women's breasts.

Charlie's dead: A euphemistic warning for your petticoat or slip is showing. An expression rapidly becoming obsolete with the changing of fashion away from wearing such items.

Charver: 1. A boy, or adolescent male.

2. A close friend, a 'mate'.

3. An unruly, young person, typically wearing casual, brand-name sportswear, such as Nike, Adidas and Reebok. Usually more associated with poorer, urban environments. Also 'charva'.

Chattin' shit: Talking nonsense.

Chat up: To talk flirtatiously with someone, to make sexual overtures.

Chav: A person, usually of poorly educated, working class origin, who dresses casually in designer sportswear and vulgar jewellery. Chavs are generally viewed as an ignorant under-class with a propensity for criminal or loutish behaviour.

Chavette: Specifically a female version of a 'chav'.

Chavtacular: Of 'chav', see above, or related them in some excessive way or major extent. Another chav related expression created during the chav obsessed early 2000s.

Chavtastic: Of, or related to 'chav'. E.g."He was wearing a Burberry baseball cap, Rockport boots, tracksuit bottoms and a fat gold chain draped around his neck - it was the most chavtastic sight to behold this year."

Chavvy:	A child.
	Of, or like a 'chav'.
Cheap as chips:	Extremely cheap. Chips, referring to French Fries, and from the period when they were considered an inexpensive meal.
Chebs:	Female breasts.
Cheeky chappy:	Affectionate name for an attractively impudent person or animal, one who may make one readily smile.
Cheeky monkey:	A light-hearted name for a verbally impertinent person.
Cheerio!:	Goodbye!
Cheers!:	1.Goodbye!, a parting salutation.
	2. Thank you!, an expression of gratitude. This is the globally accepted and most understood of the uses of cheers.
Cheese:	Smegma. Alluding to the look of this male bodily secretion and perhaps the smell.
Cheesed off:	Fed up, angry.
Cheeselog:	A woodlouse.
Cheesy:	Corny, cheap and hackneyed.
Cheesy (quaver):	1. A favour. E.g."Oh God! Do my a cheesey quaver, will you? Dont make me get up early tomorrow morning."

2. A raver, a person into the lifestyle and music of hardcore house and techno.

Cheggers: Pregnant. Rhyming slang on preggars. Also occasionally spelt cheggars.

Chelp: Impudence, cheek, especially by a child to an adult. E.g." I want you on your best behaviour when the vicar calls; any of your chelp and you'll be grounded for the week."

Chelsea tractor: A 4-wheel drive vehicle (SUV) which is used mainly in urban areas.

Chemicals: A euphemism for chemically manufactured illicit drugs, such as MDMA, Amphetamine Sulphate or LSD, as opposed to Cannabis etc.

Cherry: Virginity as in to lose one's cherry. Previously applied to the hymen but now the term is used by both sexes. One is also able to lose one's anal cherry.

Chesticles: Women's breasts, often implying either small or cute.

Chevy (chase): The face. Cockney rhyming slang.

Chewny: Chewing gum.

Chew the fat: To chat. E.g."Yeah, come round and join us, we're just chewing the fat over a glass or two of wine."

Chewy: Chewing gum.

Chib: A knife or blade. From the Romany chiv, or chive, meaning knife

1. To slash, stab or cut off.

2. To smash someone on the face with a bottle and slash with the broken shards.

Chicken: 1. A young person. Very common on the gay scene for an attractive young male.

2. A game of courage in which competitors dare one another to complete a given task. Usually a game of adolescence.

Chick flick: A film (flick), often romantic and with a happy ending, and typically enjoyed by females (chick).

Chick with dick: A male to female preoperative transexual, usually very feminine looking, with breasts and male genitals, a shemale. E.g."Last time I visited Bangkok the streets were lined with chicks with dicks, and they were so gorgeous too."

Chief: 1. A general term of address.

2. A contemptible person. E.g."I'm not sitting next him, he's a fuckin' chief and i'll likely punch him before the meeting's finished."

Chill: To relax, take time out. Abb. Of 'chill-out'. E.g."Hey calm down! You'll have a heart attack unless you learn to chill a little."

Chillax: To relax, to take time out. A combination of the words *chill* and *relax*.

Chilled: Relaxed.

Chill-out: To relax.

A time or place where people chill-out, often whilst on drugs or in a hot sweaty club.

Chill pill: Something that reduces anxiety and stress, and promotes relaxation. Mainly used figuratively in phrases such 'take a chill pill'.

Chin (someone): To hit someone on the chin. E.g."I'm going to chin that idiot if he doesn't shut up."

China: A term of address, usually friendly. Derived from the cockney rhyming slang *china plate,* meaning *mate.* E.g."Alright china! How's it going then?"

Ching: Cocaine.

Chinglish: Pidgin English, a mixture of Chinese and English.

Chinky: 1. A Chinese person.

2. A Chinese restaurant or takeaway.

Chin-wag: A conversation or chat.

To chat, talk.

Chip: To leave, go. E.g."I've just had a call from Alex; he's waiting for us at the station - we'd better chip."

Chippy: 1. A chipshop.

2. A carpenter.

Chirps: To chat up, to talk flirtatiously. E.g."I had a great night chirpsing the girls, and got the phone numbers of 3 gorgeous blondes."

Chisel: Cocaine.

Chocker: Chocolate. Also chocko or the more childlike term chockies.

Very crowded, busy. Also phrased as chocko. From the expression chock-a-block.

Chocolate drop: A black person. Offens.

Chocolate teapot: A useless thing. Usually heard in phrases such as "as useful as a chocolate teapot." E.g. "A car without wheels is as useful as a chocolate teapot."

Choice: The best, excellent. E.g."Your new boyfriend is choice; we get on really well."

Chokey: Prison.

Chonged: Very intoxicated with marijuana or cannabis. From the verb 'chong it'.

Chong it: To smoke marijuana/cannabis constantly. Possibly from the series of movies featuring the characters Cheech and Chong, both heavy marijuana smokers.

Choochie face: Affectionate term of address, often used with respect to children and babies.

Chopper: The penis.

Choppers: Teeth.

Chops: The mouth.

Chopsing: Chatting. E.g."We spent the night chopsing in the bar and didn't get to see the film."

Chopsy: 1. Chatty.

2. Moody, annoyed.

Chord A bad mood. E.g."Sarah's in a right chord after smudging her lipstick just before the photograph was taken."

Chordy Moody.

Chore To steal. From the Romany cor, to steal. E.g."You can't go choring senior citizen's pension books, it's unethical, even for a thief."

Chow Food.

1. To eat.

2. To reprimand, tell off.

Chrimble: Christmas.

Chrome dome: 1. A bald head.

2. A man with a bald head.

Chubby chaser: A person who finds fat people attractive. More commonly used on the Gay scene.

Chubbychops: Jocular and affectionate term of address for a podgy person.

Chuck: An term of endearment. E.g."Come on chuck, let's go out whilst the sun's shining."

1. To vomit. E.g."Harry's done his usual, he's missed the toilet and chucked all over the floor."

2. To terminate a relationship. E.g."I'm going to chuck her at the weekend, she's really annoying me with her moaning."

Chuck it down: To rain, often heavily. E.g."I think we should stay in and order a takeaway, it's chucking it down."

Chuck up: To vomit. E.g."I can't come to work, i've been chucking up all night."

Chud: Chewing-gum.

Chuddy: Chewing-gum.

Chuff: 1. Rubbish, nonsense. E.g."That film was boring, too long, and generally just total chuff."

2. The anus.

3. The vagina.

4. A passing of wind from the anus, a 'fart'.

Chuffed: Pleased, delighted. Compare with 'dischuffed' and 'chuffed to buggery'. E.g."I'm well chuffed at the result."

Chuffed as nuts: Extremely pleased.

Chuffer: 1. A contemptible person.

2. An annoying, difficult or disappointing occurrence. E.g."It's a right chuffer, breaking my leg just before the football season starts."

Chuffing: An intensifier, and euphemism for 'fucking'. E.g."That chuffing idiot scratched my favourite CD and now it sticks on the third track."

Chuffin 'ell: Expressing anger, surprise etc. A euphemism for 'fuckin hell'.

Chugger: A person paid to collect for charity by signing up people to make regular donations, often by direct debit. Working on busy shopping streets chuggers are often young people and will usually be seen carrying clipboards. The term is a cross between charity and mugger.

Chuggy: Chewing gum.

Chump 1. A fool, a disliked person.

2. The head.

Chunder: Vomit.

To vomit. E.g."I just made it to the toilet before I chundered."

Chung: Attractive. Mainly teenspeak.

Chunner: To mutter, grumble, talk incessantly. E.g."He's always chunnering on about nothing, he bores me silly."

Chunter: Meaning the same as 'chunner'.

Chutney ferret: A homosexual male.

Cig / ciggy: A cigarette.

Clagnuts: Faecal remnants adhering to the anal hairs or fur. Also clag nuts.

Clanger: A mistake or blunder.

Clap: Gonorrhoea.

Clap eyes on: To notice. E.g."He clapped eyes on her across the dancefloor and knew he was falling in love."

Clapped out: Worn out, broken. Usually applied to machinery. E.g."That car's just a clapped out heap of junk that needs scrapping."

Claire Rayners: Trainers (the footwear). Rhyming slang. Claire Rayner, known mainly for her role as TV/ newspaper agony aunt.

Claret: Blood. From its colour.

Clarty: 1. Sticky, gooey, messy.

2. Dirty.

Class: Of distinction, high quality, excellent. E.g."We went to the boxing last night - it was class fight that went the full distance."

Clayhead: A person from Stoke on Trent. Stoke, in the Midlands of England, is commonly called the Potteries.

Clean: Having no drugs, weapons or illicit goods on one's person. E.g."You can't arrest me officer, I'm clean!"

Clegnuts: Faecal remnants that are stuck to the anal hairs, or fur on animals. Also cleg nuts.

Clemmed: Hungry. Also spelt 'klempt'.

Clemmy: A stone or brick for throwing.

Clever-clogs: A person who is or claims to be clever or have greater knowledge. Also clever-dick.

Climb the walls: To reach a state of severe agitation through stress or worry. E.g."He's been climbing the walls waiting for his exam results."

Clingin: Unpleasant, disgusting.

Cling-ons: Excrement that adheres to anal hairs, or fur on animals. Also clingons.

Clink: Prison. It is derived either from the name of Clink Street, London, on which a prison was situated, or from the sound of doors locking.

Clinkers: Excrement that adheres to anal hairs, or fur, on an animal.

Clippie: A bus conductor. The employee, extra to the driver, who checks and supplies tickets whilst on the bus. From their clipping of tickets.

Clit: Abb. Of clitoris.

Clobber: Clothes and personal belongings.

To hit. E.g."I clobbered him over the head with a pool cue and made a break for the exit."

Clock: 1. To notice. E.g."Once I clocked him looking suspicious, he left the shop without stealing anything."

2. To hit or punch. E.g."I'm going to end up clocking that idiot if he doesn't shut his big mouth!"

Clodhopper: A large heavy shoe.

Clone: A distinct type of 'gay' image, being stereotypically masculine and epitomized by short hair, bristle moustaches, jeans or leathers. A good example being the 1970s 'gay' icons, The Village People.

Closet: The condition where one's homosexuality is concealed. 'Coming out of the closet' implying living true to one's sexuality.

Clot: An idiot, fool.

Cloth-ears: Someone who has poor hearing or doesn't pay attention to imparted information.

Clown's pocket: A large or spacious vagina.

Cludgie : A lavatory. Also shortened to cludge.

Clue up : To inform.

Clued up : Knowledgeable, informed. E.g."He's well clued up about the local music scene."

Clunge : The anus.

Clusterfuck: A disasterous situation, a mess up, a shambles.

Cobblers : An exclamation of disagreement. Derived from the noun.

Cob on: A temper. E.g."She had a right cob-on when I told her I'd spent all our holiday money."

Cock: 1. The penis.

2. A term of address, usually affectionate. E.g."Right cock, that'll be 46 pence please. Would you like it in a bag?"

3. Rubbish, nonsense.

Cocker: A friendly form of address, usually to a male. Also 'old cocker'.

Cockhead: A contemptible person, an idiot.

Cock jockey: A homosexual male.

Cock knocker: 1. A contemptible person.
2. A homosexual male.

Cockle: Ten, usually in a monetary sense. Abb. Of cockerel and hen. Cockney rhyming slang

Cock snot: Semen.

Cocksucker: A contemptible person.

Cockteaser: A person who sexually teases males.

Cock-up: A mess, a shambles.
To make a mistake, to ruin. E.g."I've cocked up again and my wife's left with the kids."

Cod: To hoax, to joke. E.g."Stop codding me and tell me the truth."

Codger: An elderly male. Usually prefixed with 'old'.

Codhead: A person from Fleetwood. A traditional fishing port in the county of Lancashire.

Cods: Testicles.

Codswallop: Nonsense.

Coffin dodger: An elderly person.

Coffin nail: A cigarette.

Coin it (in): To make large amounts of money, to profit. E.g."He's coining it now he's opened a shop on the high street."

Coke: Cocaine.

Coked up: To be intoxicated with cocaine.

Cold turkey: Withdrawal from addictive drugs and the consequential pains and discomfort, including goosepimples, hence the name.

Collywobbles: A feeling of nervousness or discomfort in the stomach.

Come: To orgasm. The common slang convention of mispelling words also gives us the variation 'cum'.

Sexually ejaculated fluid, usually applied to semen and regularly spelt 'cum'.

Come a cropper: 1. To fall heavily.

2. To fail.

Comedown: The depression and tiredness after the cessation of a bout of drug taking.

Come 'ed: Come on. Abb. Of come ahead.

Come it: To act in an impudent manner. E.g."Don't come it with me! I said you can't have any more money."

Come on: An enticement, often potentiating a relationship.

To begin menstruating. A commonly used euphemism.

Come onto: To 'chat up'.

Come out: To openly reveal one's homosexuality.

Commando Without underwear.

Commie: Abbreviation of Communist. Usually

Common: Abb. Of common sense.

Con artist: A confidence trickster.

Conflab: A chat, conversation. Also the variation confab. From confabulation. E.g."Before we set off, let's have a conflab about which route we should take."

Confuzzle: To confuse. Also confuzzled, confuzzling.

Conk: The nose.

Conkers: Testicles. A Conker (British) is the hard shiny nut of the horse chestnut tree.

Conk out: 1. To breakdown, often of machinery. E.g."I may be late, my car's conked out so I'm getting the bus to work."

2. To become unconscious.

Coon: A black person.

Cop: 1. To commune with someone sexually desirable, occasionally in so much as having sex. An abbreviation of 'cop off.'

2. To take. E.g."Cop hold of this hammer whilst I get the spanner." Also Cop this! - a facetious remark said immediately prior to an aggressive act.

3. A policeman/woman. Abb. Of 'copper'.

Value, worth. Heard in expressions such as 'no cop' or 'any cop'.

Cop a feel: Get a feel of something, often applied to a grope of a sexual nature. E.g."Is it any wonder that she reported him for sexual harrassment, he always copped a feel of her bottom whenever she walked past his desk."

Cop a plea: Plead guilty to a reduced charge.

Cop-it: To get into trouble.

Cop off: To commune with someone sexually desirable, occasionally in so much as having sex. E.g."I copped off with a gorgeous girl last night."

Cop-out: An excuse, an avoidance of guilt.

To withdraw from participation. E.g."Rumour has it that Johnny's copped-out."

Copper: A policeman/woman.

Cop shop: A Police Station.

Cop some zeds: To sleep.

Corker: An excellent thing or person.

Corking: Excellent, splendid.

Corn beef legs: Legs with mottled, blotchy skin, reminiscent of the meat, corn beef.

Corned beef: Deaf. Rhyming slang for deef, a Scottish pronunciation of deaf.

Corporation pop: Water. Dated expression.

Correctomundo: Correct. Usually as exclamation and in a patronising manner.

Corry: Abb of Coronation Street, the British 'soap'.

Cosh: A heavy stick or bar used as a weapon.

To hit over the head with a cosh.

Cost a bomb: To be very expensive.

Cotch: To relax.

Cottage: The act of soliciting illicit and anonymous sex in a public place by male homosexuals. The 'cottage' will often be a public lavatory; taking its name from when such UK conveniences looked cottage like.

Cotton on: To become aware, to notice. E.g."I cottoned on to the scam (trick) when I saw him wink at that woman."

Couch potato: A lazy person who idles away time, usually watching the television.

Cough (up): To hand over something, or reveal some information, often reluctantly. E.g. "i've already coughed up a month's wages, and can't afford any more."

Council gritter: Anus. From the rhyming slang on 'shitter'.

Council pop: Water.

Coupon: The face.

Cow: 1. A contemptible woman, a 'bitch'. Derogatory, but often used less aggressively, as an affectionate aside, as in 'silly cow'.

2. A difficult or objectionable task or thing. E.g."It was a cow of a job, and took twice as long as I expected."

Cowbag: A contemptible female.

Cowboy: A person who is unscrupulous and unqualified in business. Often with regard to 'cowboy' builders.

Cowboy outfit: A group of people, unscrupulous and unqualified in business, working under the guise of a respectable business.

Cowing Euph. For 'fucking', when used as an intensifier. E.g."That cowing bastard from the sales team got the promotion to manager."

Cow juice: Milk.

Cozzie: A swimming costume.

Crabby: Moody or short tempered.

Crabs: 1. Pubic lice.

2. The RAF (Royal Air Force).

Crack: 1. Freebased cocaine. The name derives from the sound made during its manufacture.

2. The vagina.

3. Between the buttocks.

4. As the crack, the situation, news, gossip. E.g."So what's the crack with this argument that you and Sonya have been having?"

Cracker: 1. A thing that is excellent. E.g."That West End show was a cracker."

2. An attractive person, particularly a woman.

Crackers: Crazy.

Crackhead: An addict of 'crack' (freebased cocaine).

Cracking: Brilliant, wonderful. E.g."They gave a cracking performance last night and got a well deserved 5 minute standing ovation."

Crackling: A sexually desirable woman or women.

Crack on: To progress, to go quickly. E.g."We'll crack on with the meeting after lunch."

Crack one off: To masturbate, with reference to the male. E.g."As soon as he has a spare 2 minutes, he's off to the toilet and cracking one off."

Crack on to: To come onto somebody, to make sexual advances. E.g."She was cracking on to me all night, and every other bloke at the club."

Crackpot: An insane or eccentric person.

Mad, eccentric, unworkable. E.g."I'm not going along with Suzanne's crackpot ideas."

Crack up: 1. To breakdown with laughter.

2. To mentally breakdown.

Cradle snatcher: A person who dates or marries someone considerably younger than themselves.

Crafty butcher: A homosexual male. From delivering meat via the 'backdoor'.

Crank up: 1. To increase, often with reference to the volume of music.

2. To inject drugs. E.g."He cranked up some more smack (heroin) and passed out on the floor."

Crap: 1. Nonsense, rubbish, something useless or not good.

2. An act of defecation.

3. Faeces.

Crapbag: A generally disparaging term for a person, or thing.

Crapper: A toilet.

Crappy: Rubbishy, useless, of poor quality.

Crash: 1. To share, loan or borrow. E.g."That's the third cigarette you've crashed off me in the last hour!"

2. To temporarily stay over or sleep at a place other than at one's own usual abode. E.g."Can I crash at yours tonight? It'll cost too much for a taxi home."

Crash out: To pass out due to intoxication or tiredness.

Crate: A delapidated vehicle.

Crater face: A face with pock marked skin or the person with such a face.

Craven: Greedy.

Crawl To be obsequious.

Cream: 1. To ejaculate. To cream oneself implies great sexual excitement, but often used figuratively.

2. To succeed. E.g."I thought I'd creamed my exams but I failed all but one."

Creampie: The view of recently deposited semen oozing from a vagina or anus. An expression originating in the porn industry.

Crease: The anus.

Crease up: To laugh heartily. E.g."I creased up when he spilled coffee on his suit, the next day he gave me the sack."

Create: To make a fuss, to complain. E.g."If she's going to create all night, then I'm going home to get some peace and quiet."

Cred: That which is acceptably fashionable, abb. Of credible.

Creep: A contemptible person, in particular, one who is fawning.

To act obsequiously.

Creepy-crawly: An insect, or spider, usually viewed distastefully. E.g."Don't go in the cellar, it's damp and full of creepy-crawlies."

Creps: Trainers, sports footwear.

Crewage: A gang, closeknit group of freinds. From crew.

Crib: 1. To copy, usually in an underhand or unfair manner.

2. To complain, grumble. Uncommon usage.

Crikey!: Used to express surprise or astonishment.

Crimble: Christmas.

Crimbo: Christmas. Also spelt Chrimbo.

Crimp one off: To defecate.

Cringeworthy: Likely to promote embarrassment or apprehension.

Crinkly: A geriatric person. From the appearence of their aging skin.

Croak: 1. To die.

2. To kill. E.g."I'm going to croak that idiot if he doesn't shut up soon."

Crock: Nonsense. Abb. Of 'crock of shit'.

Crock of shit: Nonsense, a worthless thing, of poor quality. E.g."Why not buy a new car? Yours is ancient, it's a crock of shit."

Croggy: A pillion ride on a single seat bicycle.

Crotch rot: General term for a sexual infection of the genitals, or venereal disease.

Crown: To hit on the head. E.g."Can you see a lump on my head? I've just crowned myself getting up."

Crozzle: To dry out and become crispy due to burning or heat. E.g."I've thrown out last night's pizza, it was all crozzled."

Crucial: Great, excellent, essential. E.g."I'm going to buy that new tune by the Kaiser Chiefs, it's crucial."

Cruckle: To twist one's ankle, to fall over on one's ankle.

Crud: Rubbish, something useless.

An exclamation of disagreement.

Cruddy: Useless, unpleasant, cheap and nasty.

Cruise: To search for a sexual encounter.

Originates from when U.S. teenagers would 'cruise' around in cars looking to pick up some company. The expression is mainly used on the 'gay' scene.

Crumbs !: A mild exclamation of surprise or amazement.

Crumpet: Sexually desirable person. E.g."The club was bursting its walls with crumpet."

Cuddy wifter: A left handed person.

Cuffy: Scruffy, unkempt.

Culchie: A rural dweller, a bumpkin, a yokel.

Culture vulture: A person keen to acquire culture.

Cum bucket: A sexually prosmiscuous woman, or similar homosexual man.

Cunning stunt: A spoonerism on stunning cunt, and adopted by users for its comic ambiguity and numerous meanings, ranging from an impressive female to an objectionable person.

Cunny: The female genitals. Derived from 'cunt'.

Cunt 1. The female genitals.

2. Women from a sexual viewpoint. Offensive.

3. A despicable person. And coarse, and with its associated

meanings is consequently particularly offensive.

Cuntchops: A general term of address, often depreciatory, and occasionally used affectionately. Also cunt chops.

Cunted: Very intoxicated by drink or drugs.

Cunt-face: A contemptible person. Also cuntface.

Cunt-faced: Very intoxicated.

Cunting: An intensifier. E.g."If this cunting weather doesn't improve within the next 24 hours we'll have to cancel the whole trip."

Cuntox: A contemptible person.

Cunt struck: Sexually besotted by a woman. Also cuntstruck.

Cunty: A contemptible person.

Cuntybaws: 1. An objectionable person.

2. Occasionally used as a term of address.

Cuppa: A cup of tea or lately also referring to coffee. The term is a contraction of cup of.

Currant bun: 1. The sun. Cockney rhyming slang.

2. The Sun newspaper. A tabloid newspaper that adopted the rhyming slang expression for its own use.

3. Son. Rhyming slang.

4. A protestant or commonly also a supporter of Rangers FC. Rhyming slang for 'hun'.

Curry-mile: The name given to an area in Manchester called Rusholme, which has a high density of asian restaurants and food takeaways positioned along its main street.

Curry queen: A gay male who is attracted to asian homosexuals.

Curtains: The end. E.g."If he doesn't make this jump, it's curtains for the whole team."

Cushy: Of an easy nature. Originates from the Hindustani khush meaning pleasant.

Cushy number: A situation that is easy and without stress.

Cushty: Excellent, fine, OK. Also spelt cushdy, and kushty.

Cut: A canal.

C-word: A coy euphemism for 'cunt'.

Cyberpunk: A nonconformist advocate of modern technology, especially such a user of the Internet.

Cyberspace: The imaginary place that exists between computers and their users, particularly on the Internet and in virtual reality.

D

Dab hand:	A person highly skilled at a given task. E.g."He's a dab hand at programming and web design."
Da bomb:	The best.
Dabs:	Fingerprints. Generally police and criminal vernacular.
Dab on:	A sweat on.
Daft:	Silly, foolish.
Daft as a brush:	Very silly, crazy.
Daftie:	A fool, an idiot.
Dagenham:	Totally insane, crazy. Because on the London underground/rail transport system Dagenham (Heathway) station is 3 stops beyond Barking station. Barking is slang for crazy.
Dago:	A foreigner, usually applied to Italians, Spanish and Portugese. Derog and offensive.
Daisies:	Boots. Rhyming slang on daisy roots.

Daisy chain: A sexual act involving 3 or more people, during which each person simultaneously has sex with the person beside them in the group, thus forming a chain.

Damage: The cost, expense. E.g."What's the damage for the meal? Without the drinks!"

Dancers: Stairs. Also, but less commonly, jolly dancers and molly dancers.

Dangleberries: Faecal remnants adherring to anal hairs.

Dangly-bits: The male genitals.

Dannies: Hands.

Daps: Plimsolls, trainers (footwear).

Dark: Excellent.

David Gower: A shower. Rhyming slang.

Deacon: An imbecile, idiot. Derived from the name Joey Deacon.

Dead: Very, extremely. E.g."Our holiday was dead good."

Dead cert: A sure thing. E.g."It's a dead cert that the favourite will win."

Dear John: A letter, usually from a female, terminating a relationship.

De-bag: To remove a persons trousers, usually without their consent. Usually adolescents behaviour.

Deck: To physically knock down, onto the deck.

Dee Dah: A person from Sheffield. Derogatory term, taken from the way they speak in Sheffield.

Deek: A look, a glance. E.g."Give me a deek at your magazine."

Deep sea diver: A five pound monetary note. Rhyming slang for fiver.

Deep shit: Serious trouble.

Deep throat: Fellatio involving the envelopment of the penis using the depth of the throat.

To fellate as in the manner of the noun.

Deffo: An abb. Of definitely.

Dekko: A look or glance. From the Hindustani, dekho.

Delhi belly: A severe stomach upset. A common occurrence for Western travellers visiting countries of the East, such as India, hence the expression.

Demic: 1. A thing that is worn out or broken.

2. A derogatory term for a person who is constantly sick, a hypochondriac, someone in obviously less than perfect health.

Destroyed: Drunk, very intoxicated with alcohol or drugs.

Devil dodger: A member of the church, or a strong believer in religion.

Devil's dandruff: Cocaine.

Dhoby: To wash, clean. Originally to do laundry, from the Hindu dhob meaning washing. Also dhobi, dobi, doby.

Dhoby dust: Washing powder.

Dial: A person's face.

Diamond: Wonderful, excellent.

Dibble: A policeman/woman. The name taken from the U.S. cartoon Top Cat, where the local policeman is called Officer Dibble.

Dibs: A claim. E.g."I put dibs on tasting it first."

To put a personal claim on something. E.g."I made the cocktail so I dibs first taste."

Dicey: Risky.

Dick: 1. The penis.

2. A contemptible person.

Dick breath: A contemptible or obnoxious person.

Dickend: A contemptible person, an idiot.

Dickfuck: An idiot, a contemptible person.

Dickhead: A stupid person, a contemptible person.

Dicksplash: A contemptible person.

Dicksplat: A despicable person.

Dickwad: A contemptible person, idiot.

Dickweed: A contemptible person.

Dicky: Unsound, likely to fail, unhealthy. Also spelt dickey and dickie. E.g."You can't seriously expect me to lift that box when you know i've got a dicky heart."

Dicky-bird: Rhyming slang for word. Usually heard in a negative sense. E.g."We've not heard a dicky-bird from Andy since he moved."

Dicky fit: An emotional outburst, a tantrum. Also dickie fit. E.g."Don't even think about smoking Angela's last cigarette, she'll have a dicky fit."

Diddicoy: A gypsy. Also spelt diddicoi and didicoi.

Diddies Women's breasts.

Diddle: 1. To have sex with, and often used with reference to masturbation of the female genitals.

2. To swindle.

Diddly: Nothing. E.g."There's diddly wrong with it."

Diddly-squat: Nothing, zero. E.g."I've earnt diddly squat this month."

Diddy: Small.

Diddy ride: A masturbatory act involving the rubbing of the penis between a woman's breasts. Also diddyride.

Diesel (dyke): A butch lesbian. A little less derogatory than 'bull-dyke'.

Dildo: 1. A substitute penis used for sex.

2. An objectionable or imbecilic person.

Dilly-dally: To dawdle, linger, loiter.

Dim: Unintelligent.

Dimbo: An idiot, a fool. From 'dim'.

Dimmock: An imbecile, an idiot. From 'dim'.

Dimp: The filter remnants of a smoked cigarette.

Din-dins: Dinner. Originally a children's expression.

Ding-a-ling: Penis. Also dingaling.

Dingbat: An idiot.

Ding-dong: An argument, commotion, fight.

Dinge queen: A gay male attracted to black homosexuals. Essentially offensive term due to the use of 'dinge', meaning black.

Dingleberries: Faecal remnants attached to one's anal hairs.

Dingy: To ignore (someone). E.g."He thought they were friends but she dingied him and went off with someone else."

Dinky: Small, cute, neat.

Dinlo: An idiot, a contemptible person.

Dip one's wick: To have sex. Male usage.

Dippy: Silly, empty-headed.:

Dipshit: A despicable person.

Dipso: A drunk, an alcoholic. Abb. Of dipsomaniac.

Dipstick: A fool.

Dirtbag: A worthless, contemptible person.

Dirtbox: The anus.

Dirty: A general intensifier. E.g."There was a dirty great big spot on the end of his nose."

Dirty-mac: A worn or decrepid long raincoat or mackintosh, the sort stereotypically worn by men with a prediliction for exposing their genitals in public.

Dirty pillows: Women's breasts.

Dirty stop-out: A person who has stayed out enjoying themselves beyond the expected time of return. Jocular usage.

Dirty weekend: A liberating weekend away from home for the indulgence in intimacies, either sexual or otherwise, with one's lover.

Dischuffed: Displeased.

Disco biscuit: An ecstasy (MDMA) pill. Within the UK club scene it was originally a specific type of ecstasy pill, however, in the U.S. in the 1970s disco biscuits were quaaludes.

Dish: 1. A sexually attractive person.

2. The buttocks. Gay use.

3. The face.

Dish the dirt: To reveal the truth or gossip.

Dish out: To hand out, distribute.

Dishy: Sexually attractive.

Diss: To disrespect, ridicule, insult. E.g."No he can't come with us - he dissed me and my family."

Div: An idiot, a pitiable person, a contemptible person.

Dive: A squalid place.

Divvy: Idiot.

Divvy up: To share out, distribute.

Dizzy queen: A giddy and flamboyant gay male.

Do: A party or event.

1. To physically assault, to beat up. E.g."I'll do him if he calls me an idiot again."

2. To have sex. E.g."I reckon i'll do her if I can get her drunk enough."

Do a bunk: To leave hurriedly, escape. E.g."He did a bunk, out of the bedroom window, when his parents came home unexpectedly."

Do a runner: Meaning the same as 'do a bunk', but often implying a departure without paying for a received service.

Dob (in): To inform on, betray.

Dobber: 1. A penis.

2. An idiot, a contemptible person.

3. Something very large. E.g."I've never seen a pizza so big, it was a real dobber, and we could only eat half of it between six of us."

4. An informer, a teller of tales. From 'dob'.

5. A condom.

Dobbing: A general intensifier. E.g."This dobbing great idiot spilt my drink and didn't apologise, so I hit him."

Doby: Laundry.

Docking: Extremely. E.g. "It was a docking big car, the size of a bus, and certainly not suitable for town driving."

Docky: A snack.

Docky time: Mid morning break.

Doddle: An easy task.

Dodgy: Risky, suspicious, dubious.

Dog: 1. A sexually unattractive person.

2. A foot, usually in plural as dogs and often heard used in the expression my dogs are barking.

To play truant. Also doggin' it.

Dog and bone: Telephone. Cockney rhyming slang.

Dog-breath: 1. A person with halitosis, bad smelling breath.

2. A contemptible person.

Dog-end: A cigarette end, the remnants of a cigarette after smoking.

Doggie fashion: An act of sex in the manner of dogs, that is, with both partners facing the same direction and on one's knees.

Dogging: Anonymous, public sex between strangers, usually taking place in cars or outdoors and in the presence of voyeurs.

Dogsbody: A person who does the menial and boring tasks.

Dog's bollocks The best. E.g."This song is the dog's bollocks."

Dog's breakfast: A mess. E.g."I've made a bit of a dog's breakfast of that essay, and will probably have to rewrite it.":

Dog's dinner: 1. A mess.

Dog's egg: A lump of dog faeces.

Do in: To beat up, to kill.

Doings: Non-specific items, things one may have temporarily forgotten the name for. E.g."Tony, will you move all your, err... Doings from the kitchen table?"

Dole: Social security benefits.

Doll: 1. A young and especially attractive woman.

2. Sweetheart. An expression of endearment, e.g. "Come on doll, it isn't that bad."

Doll up: To smarten up, to make attractive.

Dollybird: An attractive woman. Use is generally jocular and historical.

Do me a favour: A phrase meaning "you must be joking" or "are you kidding me?"

Do me a lemon: Alternative version of 'do me a favour'.

Done in: Tired out.

Dong: A penis.

Donger: A penis.

Donkey: 1. A male who is genitally well endowed, as in hung like a donkey. Also phrased as donkey-dick.

2. Something that doesn't come up to expectations. E.g."I think we've been sold a donkey."

Donnies: Hands.

Doobie: A marijuana cigarette.

Doobrie: Something whose name isn't known or has been forgotten.

Doo doo: Children's expression for faeces.

Doofah: Meaning the same as 'doobrie'. Also doofer.

Doolally: Mad, crazy, insane. A shortening of doolally tap, a madness that afflicted British soldiers in Deolali, India. There's speculation as to whether the soldiers went mad whilst stationed there, awaiting the troop ship home, or that they were sent to the sanatorium there after going mad.

Do one: To go away. E.g."Listen, I'm going to do one and let you finish your work. I'll call you later."

Do one's fruit: Vrb phrs. To be extremely annoyed. E.g."Sharon's going to do her fruit when she finds David's stuck his bloody nose into her business again."

Do one's nut: Vrb phrs. To be very angry, to throw a tantrum, to get emotionally upset. E.g."The work was piling up, he couldn't do it all by himself but the boss was doing his nut."

***Doormat*:** A person who is easily exploited, someone who is walked on and readily used by others.

Dope: 1. A stupid person. Derived from dopey.

2. General term for a narcotic drug.

***Dopehead*:** An idiot.

***Doris*:** Wife or girlfriend. E.g."I'm taking my doris to the cinema to see the new Harry Potter film."

Dork: An idiot, a contemptible person.

Dose: Euphemism for a venereal infection.

Dosh: Money.

***Do (someone)*:** To have sexual intercourse with someone. E.g."Yeah, Johnny's doing that blonde who works in the tax office."

Doss: 1. To sleep rough.

2. To rest, to idle away time. Often followed by *about* or *around*. E.g."I spent the weekend dossing around with my mates on Blackpool beach."

An easy task. E.g."That maths exam was a doss."

Dossdown: To sleep rough.

Dosser: 1. A person who sleeps rough, a homeless person.

2. A person who lives by exerting the least amount of personal effort.

Do the business: Do what is necessary to achieve the required result. E.g."If you don't do the business, we are going to fail."

Dotty: Eccentric or slightly mad. E.g."My dotty Auntie Ethel is visiting this weekend."

Double bagger: An ugly woman. So called because two bags would be needed to avoid having to see her during sex, one to cover her head, and one to cover ones own should her bag accidentally come off or rip.

Double-bubble: Double the amount.

Double Dutch: Nonsense or incomprehensible talk.

Double fuck: Used to emphasise the numerous exclamationary uses of 'fuck'.

Douchebag: A contemptible person. Also douche bag.

Dough: Money.

Doughnut: 1. An idiot, a contemptible person.

2. A skilled manoeuvre in a motorized vehicle, whereby it is repeatedly spun on the spot through 360°, resulting in the tyres overheating and consequently leaving burnt rubber on the

tarmac - in the shape of a doughnut.

Douglas Hurd: 1. A lump of excrement. Rhyming slang on 'turd'.

2. A third (class degree). Rhyming slang.

Dout: A cigarette butt.

Downer: 1. A tranquillizer.

2. Something that mentally depresses. E.g."It put me on a right downer, crashing the car, especially now when I have no money."

Down the pan: Wasted, lost, ruined. E.g."Oh well, that's another £1000 down the pan."

Down under: Australia.

Doylem: An idiot, an objectionable person. Also doylum and doilum.

Dozy Dimwitted, stupid, slow.

Drag: 1. Dressing in the opposite sexes clothes.

2. A draw on a cigarette.

Drag queen: A male homosexual who dresses in women's clothes and affecting extreme effeminate mannerisms.

Drama queen: Someone who makes an excessive fuss over a situation. Of the many queen names from the gay scene, this is regularly used by heterosexuals of heterosexuals.

Drangway: An alleyway.

Draw: Cannabis or marijuana. Also phrased as a draw. E.g."Ere mate, have you got a draw? I need something to help me sleep."

Drawk: To soak.

Dreamboat A sexually attractive male or female.

Dreckly: Immediately, straight away, although despite its meaning can also imply 'soon' or 'when ready'. From directly.

Drinky-poo: A drink. Mock juvenile expression.

Drip: A feeble and boring person.

Dripping with: Having an excessive amount of, usually in the context of wealth, such as jewellery or money.

Drippy: Ineffectual, overly sentimental.

Drive-by: The shooting of guns at a particular target from inside a car. Common with street gangs in U.S. and now occurring in Britain.

Drooth: A thirst.

Drop: To take drugs orally. The term drop acid being common.

Drop a bollock: To make a mistake. E.g."It was the third time in a week that he'd dropped a bollock. N wonder he got the sack."

Drop a clanger: To make an obvious mistake. E.g."The government dropped a clanger by ignoring the wishes of the populace and going to war."

Drop dead: An exclamation of annoyance directed at a person.

Drop one's guts: To break wind. Occasionally shortened to just 'drop one'. E.g. "Jesus! What a stink, have you just dropped one?"

Druggie: A drug addict, or more recently used with reference to anyone who uses drugs in excess; very much a subjective statement. Also spelt druggy.

Having a quality associated with that of recreational drugs and consequently the drug scene itself.

Drum: A house, home.

Drum and bass: Genre of dance music, like 'jungle', but more minimal.

Dry hump: To simulate sexual intercourse whilst fully clothed.

Dry humping: The act of simulation sex whilst fully clothed.

Dry slap: A punch. Expression supposedly invented by actor Mike Read, for the Frank Butcher character he played in a TV soap, Eastenders. E.g."You'd better show him some respect before he gives you a dry slap."

Dub:	Originally a style of 'chilled', deeper reggae music from W.Indies with added segments not dissimilar to samples.
Dubby:	Affecting the style of 'dub', but remaining within its original genre. E.g."That new dance tune I brought is very dubby."
Duchess:	A term of address for a woman. Occasionally dutchess.
Duck:	1. A term of address.
	2. A euphemism for 'fuck'.
Duckarse:	To wet the end of a cigarette, or joint, with saliva, thus making it difficult or unpleasant to smoke.
Ducker:	A stone, usually flat, used for skimming on water.
Ducky:	A form of friendly address.
Duds:	Clothes.
Duff:	Rubbishy, useless.
Duffer:	An inefficient or stupid person. E.g. "What! You went out with that old duffer ?" Derived from 'duff'.
Duff up:	To beat up.
Dugs:	Female breasts.
Duke:	A homosexual. Rhyming slang on Duke of Kent meaning 'bent'.
Dukes:	1. Hemorrhoids. Rhyming slang on Duke of Argyles, meaning piles.

2. Fists. E.g."Put your dukes up and defend yourself."

Dumbnuts: An idiot.

Dumbo: A stupid, slow-witted person.

Dump: 1. An act of defecation.

2. A squalid place.

Dune coon: An Arab, or often more generally of/from the Middle East.

Dunky: A condom.

Dunny: The toilet.

Durbrain: An idiot, fool. Also duh brain and duhbrain.

Dustbin lid: A child. Rhyming slang on kid.

Dust bunnies: Clumps of dust, usually found on the floor on the periphery of a room or under furniture.

Dutch oven: The act of breaking wind whilst in bed and then holding one's partner's head beneath the covers.

Dweeb: An imbecile.

Dwile: A dish cloth, a rag. Also, dwile flonking, a pub game played at village fetes, involving a beer soaked rag.

Dyke: A lesbian. Previously used as a derogatory expression but now used and accepted within the lesbian and gay scene. Compare with 'bull dyke' and 'diesel dyke'.

E

Eager-beaver: An enthusiastic person.

Earache: Incessant complaining or talking.

Ear bash: To talk unceasingly.

Ear bashing: A severe reprimand. E.g."She gave me a real ear bashing for embarrassing her in front of her friends."

Early doors: Early, premature.

Earner: A profitable job or enterprise.

Earwig: To eavesdrop. E.g."If you heard things said about you that you didn't like, then you shouldn't be earwigging into conversations."

Easy pink: Vaginal sex. Expression often used in conjunction with the terms *difficult brown* or *tight brown,* referring to anal sex. Euphemistic and based on references to the game of snooker.

Easy: Sexually consenting with little encouragement.

Easy-peasy:	Very easy. Usually a children's expression.
Easy touch:	A person easily exploited financially.
Eat:	A euphemism for fellatio or cunnilingus.
Eating irons:	Cutlery.
Eat out:	To perform cunnilingus.
Ecky:	The drug MDMA, Ecstasy.
Eco warrior:	An ecological activist.
Ecstasy:	The drug
Eddress:	The email equivalent of an address.
E'd up	Intoxicated by MDMA.
Eejit:	An idiot. Originally Anglo-Irish pronunciation of idiot.
Eff all:	A euphemism for 'fuck all'.
Egghead:	1. An intelligent person, an intellectual person.
	2. A person who is bald.
Eggy:	Slightly annoyed, irritated.
Elbow grease:	Manual hard work. E.g."We'll never get this finished unless you put some elbow grease into that job!"
Elevenses:	A mid to late morning drink, approximately taken at 11 o'clock.
Emmas:	Haemorrhoids. From the rhyming slang on *Emma Freud*, broadcaster, writer, and daughter of Sir Clement Freud.

Emo: Emotional.

Endz: Area, place. E.g."What endz you from?"

Eppy: Short for *epileptic fit*, however used to mean a furious uncontrollable outrage in the expressions 'throw an eppy' or 'have an eppy'. Also spelt *eppie.*

Erk: An insignificant person, and general term of contempt.

Evatch: To have. Backslang.

Evils: A hateful look. Popularized by the character named Vicky Pollard in the British comedy TV series Little Britain. E.g."Stop givin' me the evils."

Exactamundo: Exactly right, correct. Also exactimundo and exactomundo.

Expat: An expatriate.

Eyeful: A good long look. E.g."Get an eyeful of that idiot on the dancefloor."

Eyetie: An Italian. Offens.

F

Face-ache: Mildly offensive name given for a miserable looking person.

Facial: The ejaculation of semen on a sexual partner's face. Term originated within porn industry.

Fadge: The vagina. Possibly a corruption of vadge, an abb. Form of vagina.

Faff: To fuss. E.g."If you stop faffing and let me finish doing this job, then we can go out to the cinema sooner, rather than later."

Faffer: A person who fusses, or dithers.

Fag: 1. A cigarette.

2. A homosexual male. Its use isn't prevalent in Britain. Abb.of 'faggot'.

3. A chore. E.g."It was a fag having to drive all the way back home at night."

Fag bag: Homosexual male. Also fag bag.

Faggerette: A cigarette. Adolescent usage.

Faggot: 1. A homosexual male.

2. On the gay scene meaning a 'camp' effeminate male homosexual.

Fag-end: A cigarette butt.

Fag-hag: A woman who prefers the company of 'gay' men over that of heterosexuals. Fag-hags have also been known to desire sexual relations with gay men.

Fair cop: 1. A legitimate arrest. Often tongue in cheek use in expressions such as "it's a fair cop, guv".

2. A situation or event that is seen as deserved or justified.

Fair dos: An exclamation that a thing is reasonable or accepted. An extension of a fair do.

F-all: A euphemism for 'fuck all'.

Family jewels: A jocular euphemism for the male genitals, emphasising their personal importance. Not heard very often and occasionally shortened to 'jewels'.

Fancy: To like, to desire. E.g."I fancy that new receptionist who's started in accounts."

Fanjeeta The vagina, the female genitals. Also fanjita.

Fanny: The female genitals. Its use may cause confusion in the U.S. where it means buttocks.

Fanny batter: Vaginal secretions.

Fannybaws: An idiot, fool.

Fanny fart: A noise created by the genitals during sexual intercourse with the intake and expulsion of air.

Fanny fit: A fit of anger, a temper tantrum.

Fanny flaps: The female genitals, particularly the labia.

Fanny magnet: A thing that is believed to attract females. E.g."He wants a Ferrari, cos he reckons it's a sure fanny magnet."

Fannytastic: Great, excellent. Often used in a sexual context. A pun on fantastic.

Fanzine: A cheaply produced specialist magazine. A combinaton of the words fanatic and magazine.

Fapping: An act of masturbation.

Far-out: Splendid, an exclamation of approval. Jazz origins.

Fartleberry: Excrement that adheres to anal hairs or fur. E.g."You're not bringing that dog back in the house until you've cleaned him up, he's covered in fartleberries."

Farty: Insignificant. E.g."I'm not going back to that restaurant, they serve farty sized portions and I always leave still feeling hungry."

Fat-head: An idiot, imbecile.

Fat-slags: Uncouth fat women who are and look promiscuous. An expression derived from a comic cartoon of the same name in the adult and blatantly sexist comic 'Viz'. The popularity of the comic rose to phenomenal heights, hence the use of the term.

Fatso: A name for someone who is overweight or obese.

Fecker: 1. A contemptible person.

2. A person or thing. Used loosely when perhaps the person/thing is unknown to the user, and occasionally affectionate use. E.g."The poor fecker had to stay in with his wife whilst all his friends got drunk."

Feds: The police. From federal police.

Feed the pony: To molest the female genitals, in the manner of cupping one's hand to feed a horse or pony.

Feel up To sexually grope, or molest.

Felch: To lick or suck one's recently deposited semen from the rectum, or more recently the term has applied to such actions involving the vagina.

Felcher: A person who 'felches'.

Fence: A person who receives and sells stolen goods.

Fess up: To admit, to confess. Abb. of confess.

Fest: Festival. This abbreviated form is used less to mean a celebratory event, but more an eventful over-indulgence in expressions such as drug fest or beer fest.

F.H.B. Abb. Family Hold Back. A coded message for family members to delay helping themselves until guests have an adequate amount of that which is on offer, usually because of shortages.

Fiddle: To cheat.

A fraud or cheat.

Fillem A film. This north-eastern pronunciation of film is used elsewhere in a light-hearted manner. E.g."Do you fancy going to see a fillem tonight?"

Fill-in To severely beat up (someone).

Fill your boots: Help yourself! Enjoy yourself!

Be very scared.

Filth: The police. E.g."The filth are out in force tonight, so watch your behaviour and no drunkeness."

Filthy: Extremely (wealthy). E.g."She's filthy rich."

Finger:	1. To sexually molest the genitals, usually a females. 2. To inform.
Finger-fuck:	To sexually stimulate with the fingers, either the vagina or anus.
Finger pie:	The act of manually stimulating of the female genitals.
Firtle:	To appear busy but without actually achieving anything, to tinker, to do a task which is seen as a waste of time. E.g."He's been firtling in the shed all morning."
Fisticuffs:	A brawl, a fist fight.
Fitba:	Football. Scottish pronunciation.
Fit up:	To incriminate by employing false evidence. E.g."I was fitted up for that bank robbery in the high street."
Five O:	The police. Taken from the title of the U.S. TV series, Hawaii Five O.
Fiver:	A five-pound monetary note.
Fix:	A dose of narcotics to which one is addicted. However it is now also used with reference to any necessary habit. E.g."Let's call in this cafe and get a fix of caffeine."
Flabberghast:	To confound, astonish, amaze.
Flabberghasted:	Amazed, astonished.
Flake out:	To collapse from exhaustion.
Flame:	To verbally attack someone via an e-mail.

Flange: The vagina.

Flannel: Nonsense. E.g."Oh shut up! You're talking utter flannel."

To flatter.

Flash: Showy, ostentatious.

Flasher: A person who indecently exposes themselves in public.

Flash git /get: An objectionably ostentatious person.

Flash Harry: A showy and over confident young man. Dated expression.

Flash the ash: To offer a cigarette.

Flash the v's: An action of contempt, an insulting gesture. Involves raising the hand and making a V-sign with the index and forefinger, with the back of the hand facing away from the giver.

Flicks: 1. The cinema. E.g."Let's go to the flicks and watch that new British blockbuster."

2. Films, movies, videos.

Flick the bean: Of females, to masturbate. The bean referring to the clitoris.

Flid: An idiotic or objectionable person. An adolescents expression derived from flidomide, a mispronunciation of thalidomide, a drug which caused deformaties in new born babies.

Flip off: A variation and shortening of 'flip the bird'.

Flip one's lid: To lose self control, become angry.

Flipping: A euphemism for 'fucking' as an intensifier. E.g."That flipping idiot just ignored me, like I wasn't there."

Flip the bird: A dismissive, obscene hand gesture, specifically whereby the middle finger is extended from a clenched fist.

Floater: A lump of faeces that wont initially flush remains floating in the toilet bowl.

Flob: Spit, phlegm.

To spit.

Flog: 1. To sell.

2. To do with great effort. E.g."I flogged it all night to get my work done."

Floor it: To go faster, usually with respect to vehicles. From the action of pressing the accelerator pedal to the floor to increase speed. E.g."I floored it up the M6 to Liverpool, and got 6 points for speeding."

Floozie: A girlfriend or boyfriend. Orig. Expression referred to a girlfriend.

Flop To fail.

A failure.

Flower: An affectionate term of address, mainly applied to females.

Fluff: To make a mistake during a particular endevour, such as during a performance of a play. E.g."I've just fluffed my lines."

Fluffer: A person employed in the making of a porn movie, to keep the male lead sexually aroused and ready for action in-between film scenes or shots.

Flummox: To confuse, confound, bewilder. E.g."I was flummoxed by the question."

Flutter: A small bet. E.g."I'm having a flutter on the horses this afternoon."

Fly: 1. Strewd, clever, mentally alert.

2. Fashionable, stylish.

Flying fuck: Used in a phrase such as "I couldn't give a flying fuck", as a general negative statement of nonchalance.

Fly low: To have one's trouser zip/fly undone. E.g."It was so embarrassing, walking into a full conference hall, flying low."

FOAD: Go away. An abbreviation of fuck off and die, and usually written.

Fod: The forehead.

Folding:	Money, in particular higher denomination notes.
Foodie:	1. A person with a particular interest in food and things culinary.
	2. Of, or concerning food.
Fool around:	To act promiscuously.
Foosty:	Mouldy or dusty, or smelling such.
Footy:	The game of football, or a football itself.
Foreigner:	A job or work done as extra to one's usual employment and without the permission of one's employer.
Form	1. A bench. An expression from the north-west/north of England, becoming less frequently used.
	2. A criminal record.
Forty winks:	A short sleep, a cat-nap.
Four by two:	A Jewish person. Cockney rhyming slang on Jew. Can be offens.
Four-eyes:	A wearer of spectacles.
Foxtrot oscar:	Euphemism for 'fuck off'. A pun using the phonetic alphabet, therefore Foxtrot referring to the letter F, and Oscar to O, and consequently these letters as an abbreviation for 'fuck off'.

Freak-out: To become agitated with strong emotion, to traumatize. Previously when having a 'bad trip' on hallucinogens.

Freebie: Something given free, a free sample. Originally for the purposes of commerce and publicity, for example, a pre-recorded tape given away with an edition of a music magazine.

Freeload: To take or receive offered services and pleasures without reciprocation.

Freeloader: A person who 'freeloads'.

French letter: A condom. Dated expression and rarely heard.

Fresher: A first year undergraduate.

Friar tuck: Sexual intercourse. Rhyming slang on 'fuck'.

Frig: To masturbate.

An exclamation of annoyance.

Frigging: Euphemism for 'fucking', used as a general intensifier.
E.g."There's no frigging way that I'm lending you any money."

Frit: Frightened. E.g."He was too frit too complain."

Frog: A French person. The term is derived from the late 1800s when the French were known as *frog eaters*.

Frog and toad: Road. Cockney rhyming slang.

Front bottom: The vagina, the female genitals. A euphemism used mainly by females.

Fruit: A male homosexual. Only mildly offensive these days.

Fruitcake: A crazy or eccentric person.

Fuckable: Sexually desirable.

Fuck-all: Nothing. E.g."I had fuck-all to do, so I watched that new BBC sitcom instead."

Fuck-all else: Absolutely nothing. E.g."There's fuck-all else to do around here but get drunk."

Fuckathon: Sexual intercourse.

Fuck-book: A pornographic magazine or book.

Fuck buddy: A *friend* with whom one has sex, but without any of the expected or associated obligations such as sexual commitment.

Fucked off: Utterly dejected, miserable or annoyed.

Fucked up 1. Ruined, broken.

2. Distressed, mentally disturbed.

Fucker: 1. A contemptible person.

2. A person or thing. Used loosely when perhaps the person/thing is unknown to the user, and occasionally affectionate use.

3. An annoying or disappointing occurrence. E.g."Crashing my car was a real fucker."

Fuck-face: A despicable or contemptible person.

Fucking: A general intensifier. E.g."That fucking idiot deserves what he got, a black eye."

An act of sexual intercourse.

Fucknugget: An idiot, contemptible person. Also fuck-nugget.

Fucknut: An idiot, a contemptible person. Also fuck-nut.

Fuckpig: A contemptible person. Also fuck pig.

Fud: The female genitals.

Fudge nudger: A homosexual male.

Fudge packer: A homosexual male.

Full of shit: Mistaken, wrong, speaking nonsense. E.g."I'm not listening to you anymore, you're full of shit."

Full screw: A corporal in the army.

Fun-bags: Women's breasts.

Fundy: A fundamentalist, a devout religious follower. Also spelt fundi, and fundie.

Funk: A type of music that is 'funky'.

Funky: 1. Of music, earthy, bluesy and very rhythmic.

2. Exuberantly fashionable.

Funny business: Misbehaviour or deception.

Funny-farm A mental institution.

Fur-burger: The female genitals with particular allusion to pubic hair.

Fur pie: The female genitals, inclusive of pubic hair.

Furry cup: The vagina.

Fwap: To masturbate. E.g."Why should you feel guilty about fwapping whilst thinking about your best friend's mother?"

An act of masturbation.

G

Gab: To chatter, talk.

Gabba: A variety of fast Dutch 'ravey' techno.

Gabby: Talkative.

Gadge: A male, often with respect to older men. Variations include gadgy and gadgie.

Gaff: 1. Place of residence or work. E.g."My gaff is just around the corner."

2. Place. E.g."It was all over the gaff but at least I had a week to clean it up."

Gaffer: The boss.

Gaga: Insane, just a little crazy.

Gak: Cocaine.

Galoot: An ungainly and often unrefined person. Usually affectionate usage.

Gammy: Injured, painful or septic. Usually applied to a body-part. E.g."My leg's gone gammy since that fall last week."

Gan: Go. E.g."Are you gannin' down the pub tonight?"

Gander: A look. E.g."Will you have a gander at my job application letter, and check it for spelling mistakes?"

Gang-bang: Copulation with an individual by a group.

Ganja: Marijuana.

Gannet: A greedy person.

Gansie: A pullover, jumper, woollen sweater, cardigan. A corruption of Guernsey. Also spelt gansy.

Garage: Dance music not greatly dissimilar to 'house' but with a natural vocalist and more soulful. It is far less repetitive than 'house'.

Gareth hunt: A contemptible person. Rhyming slang on 'cunt'. Gareth Hunt, English actor, most famous for his role in The New Avengers television series.

Garm: Clothes. Abb. of garments.

Gary: A tablet, usually the drug MDMA. A shortening of the rhyming slang Gary Ablet; the name of a professional English footballer.

Garyboy: A male who drives a sporty car. The vehicle is usually noticeable by its sporty appearance and souped up engine.

Gary Glitter: The anus. Rhyming slang for 'shitter'.

Gas: To chat, talk incessantly.

Gash: 1. The vagina.

2. Women viewed as sexual objects.

3. Nonsense. E.g."Don't talk gash, it's all lies."

4. Rubbish, useless things.

5. Something going spare, extra, in excess of requirements. E.g. "If that's all gash, then i'll have a second helping, I'm starving."

Gasper: A cigarette.

Gasping: To be desperate for something. E.g."I'm gasping for a good night out, and a drunken few hours dancing in a club surrounded by gorgeous females."

Gatted: Drunk, intoxicated.

Gawp To stare obtrusively..

Gayarse: 1. A homosexual male.

2. A contemptible person.

Gay-boy: A homosexual male.

Gaychester: Nickname for Manchester with its ever-growing and popular gay scene. Along with 'Gunchester' and 'Madchester', these puns tend to be journalistic pseudonyms.

Gaydar: The ability, intuitive or otherwise, of a person to know when another person is also homosexual. A play on the words gay and radar.

Gaylord: A homosexual male.

Gayrage: Derogatory term for the UK garage music scene; a play on the words garage and gay.

Gazunder: A chamber pot. Named so because it goes under the bed. Somewhat archaic due to homes having internal toilets.

Gazungas: Female breasts.

Gear: Illicit drugs. E.g."Andy said he'd bring over some gear for the party, that's if he hasn't already taken it all."

Gee: Vagina.

Gee-gees: Horses. Usually children and gambler's use.

Geek: An intelligent but socially inept person.

Gennell: Alleyway, passageway between houses. A varient of 'ginnell'.

Geordie: A person from Tyneside or Newcastle, and consequently the dialect of such a person.

Geordieland: The area of Tyneside, in the North-east. Also occasionally Jordyland and Geordyland.

German helmet: The head of the penis, from its physical shape being vaguely similar to that of a German soldier's headwear.

Get a build on: To roll a 'joint', a marijuana/ cannabis cigarette.

Get it up To achieve a penile erection.

Get off on To enjoy greatly, to be thrilled, often sexually. E.g."She looked so horny; I really got off on that skin tight rubber dress."

Get one's goat: To annoy someone.

Get stuck in: Get involved in, apply oneself.

Get the horn: To be sexually aroused.

Get the nod: To get approval or permission. E.g."I've been given the nod by the wife, so will you buy me a ticket for the match on Saturday."

Ghetto blaster: A large portable stereo radio/CD/ cassette player.

Giddy kipper: An overexcitable person.

Gift of the gab: The ability to talk incessantly, persuasively, to have the knack of conversation.

Giggle: A good time, a lark.

Gilbert: A small ball of nasal mucus.

Gimboid: An idiot, a fool.

Gimmer: An elderly person. Originally the term only applied to women.

Gimp: 1. A contemptible person, a fool.

2. A sex slave, particularly one dressed in black leather apparel of a sexual nature, or similar style.

Ginger: Homosexual. Rhyming slang, from *Ginger beer* - 'queer'.

Ginnell: An alleyway, a passage at the rear of houses. Also spelt *ginnel.*

Ginormous: Huge. A combination of the words *gigantic* and *enormous.*

Gip To vomit.

Gippo: A gypsy. Also 'gypo'. Usually:

Giraffe: A laugh. Rhyming slang. E.g."You're having a giraffe if you think I'm babysitting your little brother mate!"

Girlie mag: A pornographic magazine.

Gism: Semen. Less usual spelling of 'jism'.

Give head: To perform fellatio or cunnilingus.

Give it up: To applaud, show one's appreciation. E.g."Give it up for this week's guest celebrity..."

Give out: To complain.

Glad-rags: One's finest and dressiest clothes.

Glaikit: Stupid, idiotic, usually describing a look on someone's face.

Glass: To break and smash a drinking glass into someones face.

Glass back: A fragile back or spinal area, prone to injury.

Glassback: A person with a consistently bad back.

Glesga kiss: A headbutt.

Gloopy: Viscous, sticky, usually applied to liquids.

Glop: 1. Thick viscous substance.

2. Unappetizing sloppy food.

Gloria Gaynors: Trainers, sports footwear. Rhyming slang.

Glory hole: A small hole in the dividing wall between two toilet cubicles; used for voyeurism and sexual encounters, mainly by homosexual males.

Glug: A drink of something, particularly a large mouthful.

Gnat's piss: A particularly weak and tasteless drink.

Gnat's whisker: Very close, a small amount. E.g."I missed the target by a gnat's whisker."

Go a bundle on Like, favour. Usually heard in a negative sense. E.g."I don't go a bundle on lettuce, i'll just have a cheese and tomato sandwich."

Go ape/apeshit: Become angry, furious.

Go arse over tit: To fall, to trip up.

Gob: 1. The mouth.
2. Phlegm that has been spat out. To spit.

Go ballistic: To explode with fury.

Gobbin An idiot.

Gobble: To give oral sex.

Gobby: Mouthy, offensively outspoken.

Go belly up: To fail, to go bankrupt. E.g."The company went belly up after the rise in inflation."

Gob iron: A mouth organ, harmonica.

Gob off: To talk in a opinionated and loud manner.

Gobshite: A person who talks nonsense or boasts to inflate their ego, a contemptible person.

Gobsmacked: Amazed, astounded. Originally Northern dialect but common throughout Britain from the 1980s.

Gobstruck: Amazed, shocked. Less common than 'gobsmacked'.

God-awful: Particularly unpleasant, horrible.

God botherer: A fanatical preacher of religion, an evangelist. Also Godbotherer.

Go down on To perform oral sex.

God squad: Organised religion, and its devotees, particularly evangelical Christians.

Gogglebox: Television.

Goit: An idiot, foolish person.

Go mental: To lose one's temper, go mad with rage. E.g."She went mental when she saw the stain on her beige carpet."

Gonk: An idiot.

Go off on one: To lose control. Often heard with regard to a person verbally rambling on. E.g."He had 5 grams of amphetamine and then went off on one for the next 8 hours."

Goofy: A name given to a person with large protruding teeth.

Goolies: The testicles. Originates from the Indian army during the 1800s and the Hindi goli, meaning a pellet or ball.

Goon A fool or objectionable person. Generally lighthearted use.

Gooner: An Arsenal Football Club supporter.

Goose: To poke, pinch or feel a person's bottom, usually without their consent.

Gooseberry: A person who is an unwanted extra, usually to a courting couple. From the informal expression playing gooseberry. E.g."If you two are going to spend the night kissing and cuddling on the sofa making me feel like a gooseberry, then I'm off out to the pub."

Goosey: A look. Abbreviated form of the title of the nursery rhyme Goosey Goosey Gander, making use of the word 'gander', being slang for a look.

Go postal: To go crazy, go insane. Coined after numerous incidents involving U.S. postal workers, who deranged, went on a homicidal spree before killing themselves. E.g."He went postal when that idiot smashed his car."

Goppin' Disgusting, ugly. Actually a shortening of gopping.

Gora A white person, or more specifically a white male. From Hindi.

Gori: A white woman. From Hindi.

Gorm An idiot, an imbecile. Abbreviation derived from the adjective *gormless*.

Gormless: Lacking sense, foolish.

Go spare: Become very angry. E.g."She'll go spare when she finds her best vase broken."

Goss: Abbreviation of *gossip*.

Go straight: To renounce a life of crime.

Goth: 1. A youth culture phenomenon, derivative of 'punk', characterized by black clothes, long spikey or straggly hair and dour outlook. Also descriptive of their joyless style of music. The word derives from *Gothic*.

2. A person who adopts the characteristics of the youth culture described in version 1.

Gothy: In the manner or style of a 'goth'.

Go tits-up: 1. To go wrong, to fail. E.g."Nick's devious plan went tits up when his colleagues discovered the facts."

2. To fall over. E.g."I went tits up on that ice on the path."

Go to pot: To deteriorate.

Go to the dogs: To rot, deteriorate, worsen.

Gowk: To stare obtrusively.

A fool, idiot.

Gozz: To spit. E.g."I expect it of boys but I can't bear to see teenage girls swearing and gozzing on the pavement."

Gradeley: Good, excellent. Old fashioned Northern use. E.g."That cup of tea was gradely."

Graft: 1. To work hard.

2. To steal. Criminal parlance.

Hard work.

Grafter: 1. A hard worker.

2. A criminal or drug dealer. An expression used by such members of this fraternity. E.g."It's alright, you can trust him, he's a grafter."

Grand: Excellent, lovely

A thousand pounds sterling. Orig. U.S. term for one thousand dollars.

Granny: To defeat or be defeated comprehensively. E.g."I grannied my brother in the first round of the competition, but lost in the semi-final."

Grapes: Haemorrhoids, piles.

Grasshopper: A policeman. From the rhyming slang on 'copper'.

Graveyard shift: Late night work.

Gravy: Good, OK, easy.

Greasy spoon An inexpensive and poor quality cafe.

Greb: 1. A dirty, unsavoury or contemptible person.

2. Phlegm, often consisting of nasal mucus.

Grebby: Dirty, unsavoury.

Greenie: Nasal mucus, or phlegm.

Greet: To cry, sob. E.g."We didn't get any sleep last night with the bairn (baby) greetin' until dawn."

Gregory: 1. Neck.

2. Cheque.

Gridlock: A total blockage, usually refers to a traffic jam.

Grief: Trouble, hassle. E.g."Listen, it's over! I've said sorry, so please stop giving me grief!"

Grind: A act of sexual intercourse.

To have sexual intercourse.

Grockle: A holidaymaker, tourist.

Grogan: A lump of faeces.

Grolly: Spit, a lump of phlegm.

Groovy: Excellent, wonderful. Originates in 1930s jazz speak.

Grope: To feel a person in a sexual manner. E.g."I don't care if he is my boss, I'm not being groped like that no matter how drunk I am!"

Grot: 1. Dirt, rubbish. E.g."Shall we clear out all the grot in the attic and convert it into a spare bedroom."

2. A contemptible person.

3. Sweets, confectionary.

Grotbag: 1. A dirty or sleazy person.

2. A contemptible person.

Grot mag: A pornographic magazine. Occasionally abbreviated to *grot*.

Grotty: Unpleasant, disgusting, shabby, of poor quality. From *grotesque.*

Groupie: A person who fanatically follows a rock/pop band, or celebrity, around.

Growler: 1. Vagina. From the rhyming slang *growl and grunt* meaning cunt.

2. A meat pie.

Grub: Food. Originates from the Dutch, *grubbelen.*

Grufty: Dirty, unkempt, scruffy.

Grundies: Underwear, usually applied to male underpants. Rhyming slang for *undies.*

Grunge: A type of punk/metal/thrash crossover music with its encumberment of scruffy fashions.

Grungey: 1. Scruffy, smelly, grimy.

2. Of or in the manner of 'grunge'.

Grunt: Power, when applied to machines. E.g."How much grunt has that new Porsche got?"

Gubbins: Paraphernalia, miscellaneous items. E.g."The inside of the television was full of gubbins, so I left the expert to fix it."

Guff: To break wind, to 'fart'. E.g."What's that awful smell? Has someone guffed in here?"

Gumf:	Nonsense, rubbish. Perhaps a combination of 'guff' and 'bumf'. Also 'gumph'.
Gumby:	A bumpkin, a yokel, a 'hick'.
Gunge:	Thick sticky liquid.
Gungy:	Viscous, sticky.
Gunk:	Thick gooey liquid.
Gut-rot:	Stomach ache.
Gutted:	Very disappointed.
Gutties:	Rubber soled sports shoes, trainers.
Guv:	A term of address for a man. Derived from 'governor'.
Guzzle-guts:	A person who drinks greedily.
Gym queen	A muscly homosexual male, who obviously works out in a gym.
Gypo:	A gypsy. Also 'gippo'.

H

Habdabs: Terror, the frights, nerves. A variation on the more commonly used 'abdabs'. Also occasionally *screaming habdabs.*

Hacked off: Annoyed, depressed.

Hacky: Dirty, scummy.

Hair of the dog: An alcoholic chaser which will help relieve the symptoms of a hangover, usually needed on the morning after a drinking binge.

Hair pie: 1. The vagina.

2. Cunnilingus.

Hairy: Frightening, alarming.

Hairy-arsed: Rough, primitive, unrefined, coarse. E.g."I can't imagine going out for a night at the opera with that hairy-arsed idiot."

Hairy eye: A contemptible or suspicious glance. An abb. of 'hairy eyeball'.

Hairy eyeball: A contemptible or suspicious glance.

Half-arsed: Unenthusiastic, feeble, incomplete.

Half-cut: Tipsy, drunk but not incapacitated.

Half-inch: To steal. Rhyming slang for 'pinch'. E.g."Yeah, I didn't have enough money so I half-inched it from my mum's purse."

Half-pissed: Drunk, but not incapacitated by alcohol.

Half-sharp: Stupid, dimwitted.

Half soaked: Slow witted or slow in movement, laid back.

Hames: A mess, a shambles. E.g."She made a complete hames of that meal, by overcooking the beef and making lumpy gravy."

Ham-fisted: Clumsy.

Hamilton Accie: Pakistani. Rhyming slang for 'paki'. Hamilton Accies, an abbreviation of Hamilton Academicals, a Scottish football team from Hamilton, S.E. of Glasgow.

Hammer: To take or do something to excess. E.g."I spent all yesterday hammering the booze and all last night throwing up."

Hammered: 1. Totally intoxicated.

2. Exhausted, used to excess.

Hammy: Over-theatrical. Usually applied to an actor.

Hampsteads: Teeth. From the Cockney rhyming slang Hampstead Heath, a suburb of London. Usually heard pronounced 'ampsteads.

Ham shank: An act of masturbation. Rhyming slang for 'wank'.

Hamsterdam: An intentionally jocular mispronunciation of Amsterdam.

Handbag: Style of 'house' music which has a more poppy and accessible quality, often 'crowd-pleasing'.

Hand-job: An act of masturbation. The expression usually represents the activity given by another person. E.g."She wouldn't go all the way so she gave me a quick hand-job instead."

Handle: A name, a nickname, a pseudonym, an alias.

Hand-shandy: An act of masturbation.

Hangin' Unattractive, nasty, unsavoury. Usually pronounced 'angin'.

Hang out: To reside, to loiter, to pass the time.

Hangout: A place for passing time.

Hang tough: To act tough and arrogant.

Hang-up An emotional problem, a psychological disturbance. E.g."He needs counselling to sort out his hang-ups."

Hank Marvin: Starving. From the Cockney rhyming slang as starvin'.

Hanky-panky: Sexual misbehaviour.

Happy bunny: A contented person. Usually heard used in a negative context when referring to depressed or miserable person. E.g."He's not a happy bunny, since losing his job."

Happy sack: The scrotum/testicles.

Hard: Tough and unyielding, when applied to a person.

Hard-ass: A particularly aggressive person.

Hardbag: In a further attempt to categorize 'house' music, this name was applied to 'handbag' tunes which had the hard quality of European 'hardhouse'.

Hardcore: 1. Explicit pornography.

2. A fast 'techno'/'rave' hybrid music, usually not having the subtleties of 'house' music.

Hardhead: An obstinate person.

Hardhouse: A heavier variety of 'house' music which errs towards 'techno' in its intensity and speed.

Hard-nut: An aggressive and tough person.

Hard-on An erect penis.

Have: To have sexual intercourse with. E.g."Did you have him last night or not ?"

Have a bag on: In a bad mood, angry.

Have a bog on: To be in a bad mood.

Have a cow: To have fit of anger, emotionally lose control. Often heard in don't have a cow.

Have an eppy: Have a fit of fury.

Have a face on: To appear miserable, or annoyed. E.g."I didn't speak to Wendy all morning, she had a face on and I didn't want to be shouted out."

Have arms: To fight. E.g."John's still outside, having arms with that scary looking doorman who refused him entry."

Have it: To go for it, in the sense of not holding back. E.g."We were having it last night, it was fantastic, but I can't remember a bloody thing after 3am."

Have it large: Total enthusiasm and committment to enjoyment and hedonism. E.g."We were having it large last night in town, like nobody's business."

Have it off: To have sexual intercourse.

Head: Oral sex. E.g."She gives good head."

Head-banger: A fan of rock music, usually wearing jeans and leathers. From their habit of shaking their heads violently whilst dancing.

Headcase: A lunatic, a mentally unstable person.

Headfuck: Something or someone that is mentally disturbing. E.g."I'm not inviting my sister's boyfriend, he's a headfuck and he'd ruin the party."

Head-honcho Boss. The word *honcho* derives from the Japanese *han'cho* meaning *group leader.*

Headlamps: Women's breasts.

Heap A thing that is old and delapidated. Often a vehicle.

Heavy metal: Generally, highly amplified rock music and its associated long hair and fashions.

Heavy mob:` A group of muscular or tough people gathered together to utilize their collective strengths.

Heebie-jeebies: An uneasy or very nervous feeling.

Heifer: 1. A woman.

2. A fat woman.

Hellhole: A thoroughly unpleasant place.

Helmet: The head of the penis, being similar in shape.

Hen fruit: An egg.

Hen-pecked: Under the control of a domineering female. A derogatory comment usually said of a husband.

Henry: Drug parlance for an eighth of an ounce of cannabis/marijuana. An abbreviation of Henry VIII (Henry the Eighth), a British monarch of the 1500s.

Herbert: An dull objectionable person. E.g."He's a real herbert, he watches the news and weather on TV all day."

Her indoors: One's wife.

Hick: A rustic, rural dweller.

Hickey: A love bite. Also hickie.

High: A pleasantly intoxicated state. Usually these days with regard to drug taking.

Hinglish: A hybrid language based on Hindi and English.

Hinny: An affectionate form of address. 'Geordie' pronunciation of honey.

Hip-hop Dance music genre with rapping, originating from black American street culture.

Hippyish: Of or like a hippy. E.g."I don't like all those beads, they're a bit hippyish."

Hippy: A person who adopts the characteristic style of 1960s look with long hair, worn jeans, etc., whose rejection of conventional values is often embellished with drug taking.

His nibs: A jocular and mocking title given to a self-important person.

Hissy fit: A tantrum. E.g."She had a hissy fit when I told her I'd spent all my wages on lap dancers."

Hit: 1. An injection of a drug.

2. A murder or violent crime.

Hit and miss: Urine. Rhyming slang on 'piss'.

Hit list: A list of prospective victims.

Hit the road: To depart.

Hit the sack: Go to bed.

Ho 1. A whore, a prostitute.

2. A contemptible woman. Used by extension of version 1., that prostitution is generally thought of as disreputable.

Hock: To pawn..

Hog: A powerful high handlebarred motorbike. Usually ridden by 'bikers' and 'hells-angels'.

Hoick: To lift, or move, something bulky or heavy, often with a sudden movement. Also hoik. E.g."You cant hoick that piano up the stairs, you need some rope and pulleys."

Hole: A despicable or undesirable place. E.g."You're welcome to come over to mine, but it's a bit of a hole."

Hols: Abb. of holidays.

Homeboy: A male friend or acquaintance.

Homie: A friend. Also homey.

Honeypot: The vagina.

Honk: A bad smell. E.g."It honks like shit in here, can I open a window?"

Honk up An onomatopocia for to vomit. Occasionally shortened to honk.

Honky: A white person. Generally obsolete in use, but when heard, usually jocular.

Hooey: Nonsense.

Hoof: To kick. E.g."At every opportunity I hoofed the ball up the pitch and away from our goal."

Hoo-ha: A commotion, trouble, a row. E.g."There was a right hoo-ha at work yesterday when the boss was caught kissing the office cleaner."

Hooky: Illegal, not legitimate.

Hoolivan A police vehicle, a van, with protective windscreen grills for use during riots and civil disobedience, against hooligans.

Hooter: 1. A nose.

2. A woman's breast. Usually in the plural. E.g."Cor! Look at the hooters on her."

Hop the wag: To play truant. E.g."You see far too many school kids hopping the wag."

Horlicks: A mess. Dated expression and rarely heard. E.g."I made a complete horlicks of the situation."

Horn 1. A penile erection.

2. Sexual interest or excitement. E.g."She was so sexy, I had the horn for her all day."

Horny: 1. A feeling of sexual excitement. The expression originates from the similarity between the erect penis and a horn, however it is now firmly unisexual in usage.

2. Sexually desirable. E.g."Don't you think she looks so horny in that dress?"

Hospital pass: A pass in the game of football (soccer), to a team mate whose close proximity to a member of the opposition is likely to lead to that player receiving an imediate hard tackle and subsequent injuries.

Hot air: Empty talk, nonsense.

Hot knives: A method of smoking cannabis without the aid of tobacco. A small piece of cannabis is pressed and burnt between two 'hot knives' and the resulting smoke, after being caught in a recepticle, inhaled.

Hot rocks: The red hot pieces of burning cannabis that occasionally fall from a 'joint' during its smoking.

Hottie: 1. A hot waterbottle.
2. A sexually attractive person.

Hot-wire: To start up an engine without the aid of keys.

Hoy: To throw.

Huff: A bad mood.

Huggins: Many, a large amount. E.g."I got huggins of presents for my birthday."

Hum: To smell unpleasant. E.g."Don't eat that cheese, it's starting to hum."

Humongous: Very large, enormous.

Humpty: Annoyed, irritated.

Hunk: A sexually attractive and masculine male.

Hunky: Having the qualities of a 'hunk'.

Hunky-dory: O.K., fine, erring on the side of wonderful.

Hunners: Many, numerous, hundreds.

Hurl: To vomit. Onomatopoeic as much as very descriptive of the uncontrollable force of vomiting.

Hutch up: To move up, or along, thus creating space. E.g."Michael! Will you hutch up and let me sit down?"

Hyped up Over-excited, manic.

Hyper: Over-excited, nervous, agitated.

I

Ice:	Diamonds or more generally jewellery.
Ick:	A distasteful substance. Probably derived from the adjective icky.
Icky:	Gooey or sticky, usually denoting unpleasantly so.
Iffy:	Unsound, incorrect, improbable, suspicious.
In bits:	Mentally confused. E.g."It's no wonder he's in bits, he's had two tabs of acid, four grams of coke and smoked an ounce of draw."
Indie-kid:	A person who is keen on 'Indie' music and wears its fashions.
Inside job:	A crime committed against an organisation or property, by a affiliated person.
In shtook:	In trouble. Has various spellings such as in shtuk/stook/schtuk/schtook which has been suggested comes from Yiddish.
Iron:	A homosexual. Rhyming slang on iron hoof meaning 'poof'
Item	A couple in a steady relationship.
Ivories:	Teeth.

J

J: A marijuana/cannabis cigarette. Abb. of 'joint'.

Jab: A hyperdermic injection, a vaccination. E.g."You don't need hepatitis jabs to visit Cornwall, it's not a foreign country."

Jack: To steal, often in relation to mugging. From hijack.

Jack all: Pron. Nothing. E.g."There's jack all wrong with it."

Jack and danny: Vagina. Rhyming slang on 'fanny', slang for vagina. E.g."What, with her short skirt, and no knickers, I had great view of her jack and danny."

Jack and jill: A pill. Cockney rhyming slang.

Jackanory: 1. Story.

2. A lie, a tall story.

Rhyming slang on story.

Jackbit: Food, or more specifically a packed lunch.

Jacking off: An act of masturbation.

Jack off: To masturbate. Usually applied to males. E.g."I jacked off to the thought of her completely naked apart from wearing a pair of white cotton pants."

Jack shit: Pron. Nothing.

Jacksie: Buttocks, or anus.

Jack's alive: Five. Rhyming slang.

Jack-the-lad: A male who is quick witted, a rogue who looks out for themselves.

Jack-up: To inject with drugs.

Jaffa: An infertile male. From jaffa oranges being seedless. This term either gained prominence from or was invented for the British TV sitcom Only Fools and Horses in the 1990s.

Jag: An injection.

To prick.

Jailbait: An attractive female or male who, viewed sexually, is younger than the legal age of sexual consent. Also jail bait. E.g."I'll warn you now, dont get involved with Mike's sister, she's jailbait."

Jake/jakey: 1. A drunk, a meths drinker.

2. A down and out, a homeless person.

Jam jar: A car. Rhyming slang.

Jammy: Fortunate, lucky.

Jam packed: Full to capacity.

Jam rag: A sanitory towel, a tampon.

Jam roll: 1. An idiot.
2. Anus.

Jam sandwich: A police car, specifically the white ones with a bright red band running horizontally along the sides.

Jam week: The period of menstruation.

Janner: A person from Plymouth.

Jap's eye: The urethal opening on the head of the penis.

Jar: A glass of beer or lager, usually a pint.

Jarred off: Upset, fed-up.

Jasper: A wasp.

Jazz mag: A pornographic magazine.

Jellies: Cheap rubber/plastic sandals mainly worn by children. Their transparent and brightly coloured appearence resembles jelly, hence their name.

Jellyfish: A weak and ineffectual person.

Jerk: Idiot.

Jerk-off: To masturbate. E.g."He's in his room, jerking off to that new adult film he brought."

Jerry: 1. A German, or from Germany, often in a military context.

2. A chamber pot. Dated.

Jessie: A feeble, easily scared person, a softy.

Jesus boots: Sandals.

Jesus freak: A strong believer in Christianity.

Jet: To move quickly or depart hurriedly. E.g."I'm just gonna jet into town to collect my holiday money."

Jiffy: A moment, a short time. E.g. "Wait there a second, i'll be back in a jiffy."

Jigger: An alleyway, back passage.

Jiggered: 1. Confounded. Heard in the rather archaic exclamation, i'll be jiggered!

2. Worn out, exhausted.

Jiggery pokery: Deception, trickery, dishonest behaviour.

Jiggy: Cool and in touch with what's happening and respected. Apparently originates with Will Smith, U.S. rapper and movie star, and came to prominence with his song Gettin' Jiggy Wit' It.

Jill off: Of women, to masturbate. Expression punning and created as a female equivalent to 'jack off'.

Jimjams:	Pyjamas. Also 'jim-jams'.
Jimmy hill:	A pill. Rhyming slang. Jimmy Hill - football player, manager and then TV sports presenter.
Jip:	Hassle, bother.
Jism:	Semen. Also 'gism'.
Jitters:	Severe nervousness.
Jizz:	Sperm. Abb. of *jism.*
Joanna:	Piano. Cockney rhyming slang.
Jobby:	1. A lump of excrement. 2. An act of defecation. E.g."Give me 5 minutes, i've just got to have a jobby."
Jobsworth:	A person who is very pedantic at work and strictly adheres to the rules; so called because of their oft used exclamation, "I can't let you do that, it's more than my job's worth."
Jock:	A Scottish person. Can be offensive.
Jockey's whips:	Chips, French fries. Rhyming slang from the North-west.
Jodrell:	An act of masturbation. From the rhyming slang *Jodrell Bank* - *'wank'*. Jodrell Bank, a large radiotelescope in Cheshire, North-west England.
Joe Baxi:	Rhyming slang for taxi.

Joe Bloggs: A fictitious name for the average or unknown person.

Joey: 1. A friend or acquaintence who is regarded a fool or weakling, and often has to bear the brunt of jokes. Believed to be derived from the rhyming slang *Joe Hunt,* meaning 'cunt'.

2. An imbecile. Derived from the name *Joey Deacon*, a physically handicapped (cerebral palsy) guest on a British children's TV programme called Blue Peter in the 1970s; consequently his name was cruelly adopted by children as an insult.

Johnny: A condom. Derives from the term French Letter via the archaic slang Frenchie and consequently Johnny Frenchman.

Joint: A cannabis or marijuana cigarette.

Jollies: 1. Pleasure, thrills. E.g."He always gets his jollies from hurting others."

2. Holidays, vacation. E.g."Are you going to mainland Europe again for your jollies?"

Josh: To jest and joke with someone. E.g."Dad! Stop joshing me. She's not my girlfreind, just a mate."

Joyride: A ride in a stolen vehicle.

To go on a joyride.

Jubblies: Women's breasts.

Jug handles: Ears, usually implying large or excessively protruding.

Jugs: Breasts.

Jumbly: 1. A jumble sale.

2. The unwanted goods and possessions which are sold at a jumble sale.

Jumped up Arrogant.

Jungle: A dance music based around speedy 'breakbeats', 'dubby' bass and 'samples'. It originates from rave and hardcore dance music.

Jungle bunny: A black person.

Junglist: A person interested and committed to 'jungle' music.

Junkie: 1. A heroin addict. Also spelt *junky*.

2. Now more frequently used for anyone with an addiction.

K

Kak:	1. Rubbish, nonsense.
	2. Excrement.
Kankles:	Fat ankles and calves that lack definition and appear to merge. A combination of the words *ankle* and *calf*. Usually spelt 'cankles'.
Kaylied:	Very drunk. Also spelt *kalied*.
Keep it zipped:	Don't talk, stay quiet.
Keep tabs on	To keep informed about.
Kegs:	1. Trousers.
	2. Men's underwear.
Ken:	To know.
Kerb crawler:	A person who drives slowly to view street prostitutes, with the intention of procuring their services.
Kerfuffle:	A commotion or fuss. Also occasionally spelt *cafuffle, cufuffle* and *curfuffle*.
Ket:	Sweets, confectionary, candy.

Kettle: A watch or wrist watch. Possibly from rhyming slang *kettle and hob,* meaning *fob.*

Kev: A young person who typically wears branded sportswear, baseball caps, trainers or Rockport boots, etc.

Kev car: A modified car, including such things as alloy wheels, spoilers, loud sound systems etc.

Kevved up: Typically with reference to a car, mechanically and performance enhanced, restyled to look extra sporty.

Kewl: 1. Excellent, wonderful.

2. OK.

Kibosh: To end, to terminate, to finish off. E.g."We were kiboshed as soon as we set off."

Kick in To begin. E.g."The drugs kicked in just as I was talking to my boss. I made a quick exit."

Kickin' Full of life and energy. E.g. " The club was kickin last night."

Kick it: To die. A shortening of *kick the bucket.*

Kick off: To start trouble. E.g. "If we don't keep the noise down he's going to kick-off again and call the police."

Kiddo A form of address, for a younger person than oneself. Often used affectionately.

Kidology: The persistent and intentional deception and teasing of someone for pleasure.

Kike: A Jew.

Kipper: The face. E.g."Did you see the miserable kipper on that idiot stood at the back?"

Kiss arse/ass: To act obsequiously.

Kisser: Mouth. Origins in boxing.

Kite: To fraudulently use dud or stolen cheques. E.g."I got some fantastic sportswear this morning, kiting in the precinct."

A person who passes dud or stolen cheques.

Klempt: Hungry. Also 'clemmed'.

Klepto Abb. of kleptomaniac.

Klingon: Faecal remnants that have adhered to anal hairs. Unusual and less common spelling of 'clingon', possibly inspired by the Klingons from the Star Trek TV/film series.

Knacked: Means the same as 'knackered'.

Knacker: To wear out, to exhaust, to ruin. E.g."Keep hitting it with that hammer and you'll knacker it."

Knackering: Tiring, exhausting. E.g."Climbing to the top of the Mount Everest was the most knackering thing I have ever done."

Kneecap: To cripple someone by shooting or hitting their kneecaps as a means of punishment.

Knees-up: A lively party.. E.g."There's going to be a knees-up at Jenny's tonight, it's her birthday."

Knee trembler: Sexual intercourse whilst standing. Usually hurried sex in an attempt to grab the moment.

Knob: 1. The penis.

2. An idiot, an objectionable person.

Knobber: A contemptible person, an idiot. Also *nobber*.

Knobbing: Sexual intercourse. Also 'nobbing'.

Knob-end: 1. The head of a penis.

2. A contemptible person.

3. The very end of something. E.g."Ok, i'll eat the knob-end of the bread, the crusty bits are my favourite."

Knob-head: An idiot, a contemptible person. Also *nobhead*.

Knob-shiner: A contemptible person.

Knocked up: 1. Tired, exhausted.

2. Pregnant.

Knockers: Breasts. Possibly named due to the nature of their movements during activity.

Knock-off: 1. To have sex with (someone). E.g."She's just not my type, but I'd definitely knock off her sister."

2. To steal.

3. To stop work. E.g."We knocking off for lunch in 10 minutes, so finish what you're doing."

Knock one out: Usually of males, to masturbate. E.g."He knocked one out whilst watching old episodes of Baywatch."

Knock up 1. To make pregnant. E.g." I knocked her up and now her father wants me to marry her."

2. To awaken.

Kooky: Crazy, eccentric.

Kopite: A supporter of Liverpool football club. From *The Kop*, a stand/area at the Liverpool ground.

Kosher: Correct, legitimate.

Kraut: A German. A shortening of *sauerkraut*.

Kushty: Excellent, fine, OK. Also spelt *cushty* and *kushti*. A once predominantly working class term with origins either in the Middle East and/or Romany

L

La:	A form of address unique to Liverpool. Its prevalence is generally perpetuated by stereotypical 'scouse' impersonations by outsiders; younger generations from Merseyside tend not to utilize this expression. Pronounced *lah.*
Labs:	Abbrev. Of labia.
Lace into	To attack, either verbally or physically.
Lacky-band:	A corruption of the words elastic band.
Lad:	Penis. Affectionate use. E.g."I'm going to the clinic this afternoon, my lad's not been right after that shag with your sister."
Laddette:	A female equivalent of a male who might be considered 'laddish'. Such characteristics might be confident, brashness, loudness, sexism, enjoyment of drinking etc.

Laddish: Of or like the characteristics of a young man or lad, often loud, macho, arrogant and sexist.

Ladyboy: A male to female part transexual.

Lady garden: The female pubic area, the vagina and pubic hair.

Lady Godiva A five pound note. Rhyming slang for *fiver*.

Lager boys: Young men who over-indulge in alcohol and consequently become loutish.

Lager lout: A young person whose anti-social behaviour is primarily instigated by the excessive drinking of alcohol.

Laik: To play. Also leck. E.g."Are your two brothers laiking out this afternoon, because i've got a new football for my birthday?"

Lambchops: Sideburns. From their shape?

Lamp To hit, to clout. E.g."I can't believe she lamped him. Just for coming home drunk."

Large it: To be enthusiastic.

Lark: An activity one considers a waste of time. E.g."I'm not at all comfortable with this abseiling lark; the climbing up is alright but coming down backwards, now that's stupid!"

Laughing gear: The mouth.

Lav: A toilet. Abb. of lavatory. Also *lavvy.*

Lay: To have sexual intercourse. E.g."I got a little drunk last night and got laid."

Leathered: Drunk:

Lech: To sexually lust. Also spelt *letch.*

Someone who is lecherous and lustful.

Lecky: Electricity. Also 'lecko'. E.g. "I'm afraid we can't invite you back, we've had the lecky cut off."

Leftfield: Taking an unconventional view or stance.

Left footer: A Catholic.

Lefty: A socialist.

Leg it: To run hurriedly. E.g."We heard the police sirens and legged it."

Legit: Abb. of legitimate.

Legless: Very drunk. Obvious derivation from the consequences of excessive alcohol.

Leg-over: Sexual intercourse, usually in phrase 'get one's leg over'. E.g."Did you get your leg-over with that girl last night?"

Lemon: 1. A fool, idiot, objectionable person.

2. A lump of excrement. Rhyming slang on *lemon curd*, meaning 'turd'.

Lemon squeezy: Easy, simple. Either from the rhyming slang or the juvenile rhyme - *easy peasy, lemon squeezy.*

Leo An all day drinking spree. From the rhyming slang *Leo Sayer - all dayer.* Leo Sayer, a British pop music artist during the mid 1970s.

Lesbo: A lesbian.

Let off: To break wind, to 'fart'. Shortening of *let off wind.*

Let one go: To break wind, to fart. E.g."That's disgusting! Who's just let one go?"

Lezzer: A lesbian.

Lick arse: To act obsequiously, to be a sycophant.

A sycophant.

Lickle: Small. A lazy or childlike corruption of the word *little.*

Lick up To fawn, to be obsequious. E.g."She licked up to the teacher and got a grade A in her English language test."

Ligger: A 'freeloader', a taker of things that are freely available, especially in the world of show business or music.

Like a bastard: In a hurried or agitated state. E.g."I raced around the shops like a bastard, looking for a birthday present."

Lilly: The police. From Polari slang *Lilly Law*.

Lils: Breasts.

Limey: An English person. Derived from the habit, on long journeys, of supplying lime juice to English sailors as a preventative against scurvy.

Limp-wristed: Feeble, effeminate, usually applied to males, and often implying homosexuality.

Line: A quantity of powdered drug, such as cocaine, that is chopped and presented as a line to be snorted.

Lionels: Flaired trousers/jeans. Rhyming slang on Lionel Blair's, meaning flairs. From the British dancer/ entertainer, Lionel Blair.

Lippy: Impertinent, mouthy, cheeky.
Lipstick.

Lips: The labias.

Lipstick lesbian: A lesbian who prefers to wear make-up and look conventionally feminine, as opposed to 'bull-dyke' or 'diesel-dyke'.

Liquid lunch: A lunch break comprising of alcohol instead of food.

Little fella	Affectionate term for an ectasy pill. E.g."We cant have a good night tonight until we get some little fellas."
Littles:	Pills, or more commonly ectasy pills.
Load:	The quantity of semen that is usually ejaculated. E.g."She was so horny I shot my load just looking at her."
Loaded:	1. Drunk, or drugged up. 2. Wealthy.
Lob on	An erect penis.
Lobster:	A very sunburnt person.
Lock-in	The time after a public house has closed when a chosen few are offered the chance to buy more drinks. An illegal activity, hence the locking of doors.
Log:	A lump of excrement. From its vague similarity to a to a sawn tree trunk.
Lolly:	Money.
Long-hair:	A hippy.
Loo	A lavatory.
Lookah:	Money. It is derived from *lucre,* a derogatory ter[illegible] profit or gain. Also spelt *luka.*
Looker:	An attractive person.

Loon: An insane person. Abb. of lunatic.

Loopy: Mad, insane.

Lord Muck: The depreciatory name for a pompous conceited man. The female equivalent being Lady Muck.

Lose it: To become confused or out of control.

Lose one's rag: To lose control in a fit of fury, to be very angry. E.g."You should keep out of Jill's way when she loses her rag; she's got a lethal right hook."

Lose the plot: Be confused, to go off direction, whether with conversation or in one's activities.

Lounge lizard: 1. An idle frequenter of fashionable bars.

2. Someone who is very lazy and unenergetic.

Louse: To finish a job or task.

Love: A friendly term of address.

Love custard: Semen.

Loved up: 1. In love.

2. High on drugs and feeling intimate and empathetic, usually on MDMA.

Love handles: An area and build up of fat on a person's waistline.

Lover boy: 1. A lover, an attractive man.
2. A friendly term of address.

Love spuds: Testicles.

Low-life: Contemptible and despised person or persons, often with criminal leanings. E.g."I'm not going in that bar, it's full of low-life and I value my own life."

Lug: Ear.

Lumber: To burden. E.g."What am I, a doctor? Don't lumber me with all your medical problems, go to the medical centre."

Lummox: A clumsy, stupid person. Often used affectionately.

Lunchbox: Male genitals.

Lungs: Women's breasts.

Lurgy: Any unspecified or indeterminate illness. Jocular use. Also *lurgee.*

Lurve: *Noun*/Love. Humourous and intentional mispronunciation to suggest more passion and lust.

Lush: Excellent, appealing, attractive.

A habitual, heavy drinker of alcohol.

Lusty: Sexually excited. Derived from the s.e. *Lust* and grammatically correct adjective *lustful.*

Lychees: Testicles.

M

Maccy d's: mcdonalds, the fast food company. Also occasionally *Macky d's*.

Mad aleck: A person acting crazily and energetically. Usually heard applied to overenergetic children by parents or guardians. Also spelt *mad alec* and *mad alick*.

Made up: Happy, very satisfied. E.g."I'm made up about your good news."

Mad hot: Extremely hot.

Mad keen Very enthusiastic.

Mafted: Of a person, hot and bothered, oppressed by heat. Also *mafting*, pronounced *maftin'*, relating to hot and humid weather.

Maftin: Hot and humid. E.g."Oh God! It's maftin. Can we go swimming today."

Maggot: 1. A despicable, devious or obsequious person.

2. A small penis.

Mahusive: Immense, sizable, great. Probably from *massive.*

Make a row: To make a loud noise. E.g."I've got such a headache, the kids have being making a row all afternoon."

Make it snappy: To hurry up, to do it quickly. E.g."Steve, the film starts in 5 minutes, so if you are going to wash your hair you better make it snappy."

Hurry up!

Make tracks: To begin a journey. E.g."OK, it's 8.30 and we've got to get to London by midday, let's make tracks."

Mam Mother. A less common variation on *mum.*

Manc: A person from Manchester, England. Abb. of Mancunian.

Man-fat: Semen.

Manashee: A woman. Female equivalent of 'gadge'. Also *manishee.*

Manky: 1. Scruffy, dirty, distasteful, disgusting.

2. Poorly, unwell. E.g."I'm not coming into work, I feel a bit manky."

Manmuck: Semen.

Manor: The home district felt to belong to a person or gang.

Man tits: Male breasts.

Map of Tassie: The vagina, inclusive of pubic hair. From the similarity of the external female genitals to Tasmania. Popularized in the UK by the comic Viz.

Mard: 1. A weak willed person, a softie.

2. A bad mood or temper.

Mardarse: A weak willed person, a softie.

Mare: 1. A woman. E.g."You silly mare! Why did you do that?"

2. A terrible situation. Abb. of *nightmare*. E.g."We had a mare of a journey and got stuck in the traffic jams on the M25."

Marra: A mate, friend, 'pal'.

Mars bar: A scar. Rhyming slang. E.g."He was a really sensitive lad, despite that Mars bar making him look mean."

Mash: To brew a cup of tea.

Mashed: Utterly intoxicated by drink or drugs to the extent of being in a mess and unable to function normally.

Massive: A group of people closely united by community and social interests and usually defined by geographical area, e.g. Moss Side Massive.

Mate: 1. A friend.

2. A form of address.

Mazed: Mad, insane.

Meat: Sexual organs.

Meat-head: A term of abuse, with the implication that the recipient may have more brawn than brains.

Meat injection: An act of sexual intercourse.

Meat market: A place or event where the objective of a sizeable number of those frequenting is to find sexual partners. Often used with regard to nightclubs.

Meat wagon: 1. A police van.

2. An ambulance.

Me duck: A form of address. Actually *my duck*.

Mee maw: To pull faces. From the exagerrated expressions made on the faces of conversing mill workers, in an attempt to make themselves understood over the din of machinery.

Meff: A scruffy, unkempt person, and consequently an objectionable person.

Megabucks: A huge quantity of money. The term is used despite the expression 'bucks' (money) remaining firmly an Americanism.

Melons: Breasts. The term usually refers to large breasts.

Melvin: When ones trousers become caught up between ones buttocks.

Member: The penis. Assumed to be from the latin *membrum virile.*

Mental. Insane, crazy.

Mentalist: A crazy person, a mental case.

Merkin: An American. A pun on the word *American* sounding similar to *a merkin.* From the s.e. Merkin, a pubic wig.

Mersey trout: A lump of faeces. From when the River Mersey was very unclean and poluted.

Messages: Groceries, usually heard in *do the messages,* meaning buy the groceries.

Mess around: A euphemism for noncommittal sexual relations.

Mick: An Irishman. From the popular Irish name, Michael. Generally offensive.

Middle leg: The penis.

Miffed: Annoyed, peeved. From the informal/colloquial verb *miff.*

Milf: A sexually desirable and mature woman. An acronym of *Mom I'd Like* to *Fuck.* If not invented for the film *American Pie,* then certainly popularized by it.

Milkers: Women's breasts.

Minced: Drunk, intoxicated.

Mince pies: Eyes. Rhyming slang.

Mincer: A homosexual male. From the S.E. *mince,* an affected manner of walking.

Mincers: Eyes. From the Cockney rhyming slang 'mince pies'.

Mind-blowing: Totally astonishing or confusing. The term is derived from the drug culture of the 1960s.

Mindfuck: A situation or person who gives one an mentally overwhelming and disorientating experience.

To mentally confuse and overwhelm.

Ming: To smell or look unpleasant. E.g."Yearghh, that's disgusting! It mings in here! Which one of you has farted?"

Minge: The female genitals. Derived from dialect, which ultimately may have its roots in the Romany, *minj.*

Mingebag: 1. A despicable person.

2. A miser.

Minger: A physically undesirable, smelly, or ugly person. Pronounced with a hard G. E.g."It wasn't 'til we woke, the next morning, that I realised quite what a minger she was. I left pretty damn sharpish before she asked for my phone number."

Mingy: Miserly, stingy. E.g."Don't be so mingy, share the chocolate with your sister."

Mint: Excellent, wonderful.

Minted: 1. Wealthy. E.g."Just because he's minted doesn't mean he's upper-class."

2. Excellent.

Minty: Scruffy, dirty.

Misery-guts: A killjoy.

Misog: A grumpy old man. Acronym of *miserable old git.*

Mits: The hands. E.g."Get your mits off my sandwich you thieving swine."

Mo: Abb. of moment. E.g."Just a mo, wait there and i'll be with you in one minute."

Mob-handed: In large numbers, en masse, with respect to people. E.g."We went down there mob-handed and made sure they understood that it wasnt worth starting a fight."

Moby: A mobile phone.

Sick, ill. Rhyming slang on Moby Dick.

Mod cons: Abb. of modern conveniences. Also *all mod cons.* E.g."The house was large and well kept, but it lacked mod cons such as a flushing toilet."

Mofo: A contemptible person. Abb. of 'motherfucker'.

Moggie: 1. A cat. Also spelt moggy.

2. A mouse.

3. A Morris Minor (car).

Moneybags: Someone who freely displays their current wealthy status.

Money shot: The male orgasm shot, that usually determines the end of a sex scene in a pornographic film. Originally porn industry terminology.

Monkeyhanger: A person from Hartlepool, in the North-east of England.

Monkeytown: Nickname for the town of Heywood, Lancashire.

Moo: An objectionable woman

Mooch: 1. To idle away time, to loaf around.

2. To amble along, to casually walk.

Moody: Suspicious, not genuine. E.g."Don't buy any watches off that crook, they're well moody."

Moo juice: Milk. From *moo* meaning *cow*.

Moolah: Money.

Moose: A physically unattractive person. Used frequently from 1990s.

Mopper-upper: A person or thing with the job or task of mopping up.

Moresome: Group sex, usually implying the number of participants being greater than 3 (threesome).

Mornge: A whingey, feeble person.

Morngy: Moany, whingey, feeble. Also *morngie* and *mawngy*.

Morning glory: A erection of the penis on awaking from a night's sleep.

Mortalled: Drunk, intoxicated.

Mosey: A look around. E.g."I'm just going to have a mosey around the shops."

Moshpit: An area immediately infront of the stage at gigs where 'moshing' occurs.

Mosquito bites: Small breasts.

Motherfucker: A contemptible person. Occasionally shortened to *mother*.

Motoring: Proceeding quickly. E.g."Now we have some up to date machinery we are motoring through the work schedule."

Mott: Vagina.

Mouse: A female's sanitary tampon. From the vague physical similarities, i.e. Having a body, tail, and from being white.

Mouth off: To talk loudly and without thought.

Mozzy: Mosquito. Also *mozzie*.

Muck in: To join in and assist in an activity or task.

Muck-up A bungled event. E.g." That social around at Bill's last week was a right muck-up."

Mucky: Rude.

Mucky pup: A dirty person, affectionate use and often applied to a child. E.g."Look at the state of your clothes, you mucky pup! You've been rolling around in the dirt with Billy again, haven't you?"

Muff: The female genitals. The innuendo being inclusive of pubic hair.

To spoil or fail. E.g."She muffed her chances of winning the race when she stumbled at the last hurdle."

Muff-dive: To perform cunnilingus.

Muff diver: 1. A person who indulges in cunnilingus

2. A lesbian.

Muffin: An idiot, fool. E.g."She made me look like a right muffin telling her friends about my yellow polkadot underwear."

Mug: 1. A stupid or gullible person.

2. The face. E.g."Get your ugly mug out of my house, now!"

3. The mouth.

Muggins: A fool, someone easily outwitted, usually said with regard to oneself. E.g."That's right, leave it to muggins here, as usual i'll do the washing up."

Mug's game: A foolish activity. E.g."You won't get away with stealing cars for long, it's a mug's game."

Mug-shot: A photographic portrait. Often with regard to a police photo of a criminal or suspect.

Mullered: 1. Drunk, intoxicated by alcohol.

2. Physically beaten up.

3. Beaten, in competition. E.g."We got mullered in the football final."

Mullet: A style of haircut, shorter at the top and considerably longer at the sides and back.

Munch: Food, a snack. E.g."Can we stop at the next cafe and get a munch?"

Munchies: 1. The urgent hunger experienced after having smoked cannabis or marijuana.

2. Food, usually for snacking.

Munted: 1. Ruined.

2. Very drunk or intoxicated with drugs.

Munter: An ugly person, usually applied to women. Also spelt *munta.*

Muppet: An idiot, an objectionable person.

Murder: To consume greedily. E.g."I'm so thirsty I could murder a cup of tea."

Muscle: A collective term for sizeable and strong people, gathered to utilize their strengths.

Muscle Mary: A muscular, homosexual male.

Mush: 1. The mouth. E.g."Shut your mush you noisy git!"

2. A term of address, usually used to attract the attention of a stranger. Derived from the Romany for man.

Mushies: Abb. of mushrooms.

Muso A musician or person particularly interested in music.

Mutant: A foolish or objectionable person.

Mutton Deaf. Abbreviated form of the rhyming slang 'mutt'n'jeff'.

Mutt's nuts: The best, the most excellent. A variation on the earlier expression, the 'dog's bollocks'.

N

Nab: 1. To steal.

2. To arrest. E.g."Charlie's been nabbed with his hand in the till again."

Nadgers: Testicles.

Nads: Testicles. Derived from *gonads*.

Naffed off: Annoyed, depressed.

Naff off: Get lost! Leave me alone! A euphemism for 'fuck off!'.

Go away. E.g."Will you naff off and leave me to get on with my work."

Nail: 1. To have sexual intercourse with. E.g."Did you nail that girl you were all over in the club last night?"

2. To seduce.

Nan: Grandmother.

Nana: 1. Abb. of banana.

2. A fool or idiot. Jocular usage.

Nancy: 1. An effeminate male.

2. A homosexual.

Effeminate, weak.

Nancy-boy: A homosexual male.

Nang: Excellent, great.

Nark: 1. An informer, particularly a police informer. From the Romany *nak,* meaning nose, in the sense of sniffing out information. Not from *narcotics* agent, a mid 1900s job and title, as often mistakenly believed.

2. A bad mood. E.g."He was in a total nark after getting yet another parking ticket."

Narked: Annoyed, ill tempered.

Narky: Annoyed, moody, upset.

Natch: Naturally, of course. Abbreviated form of *naturally.*

Natty: Smartly and stylishly dressed.

Naughty bits: A coy euphemism for the genitals.

Nause: An annoying or irritating, person or thing.

Neat: A general term of approval, such as excellent, 'cool'.

Nebby: Nosey (or nosy). From 'neb'.

Needle: To make jibes at, irritate.

Needle dick: 1. A small penis.

2. A man with a small penis.

Nellie: 1. An effeminate or homosexual male.

2. A feeble, soft person.

Nerd: 1. An imbecile, contemptible person.

2. An intelligent, obsessive and often socially inept person, typically thought of as boring or dull. The expression is often associated with technically minded computer users.

Nesh: 1. Over-sensitive to cold, when applied to a person. E.g."I suppose you want me to turn the fire on, being so nesh."

2. Cold, with respect to the weather. E.g."Put your coat on Billy, it's nesh outside."

Net-head: A person obsessed with using the internet.

Nibbles: Small snack type food, especially when eaten before a meal or with drinks.

Nicker: One pound sterling. Also spelt 'knicker'.

Niff: A bad smell.

Nifty: 1. Stylish. E.g."The car's looking loads more nifty with that rear spoiler and go-faster stripe."

2. Quick and agile.

Niggly: Peevish, bad tempered.

Nimps: Easy, simple.

Ninny: A foolish person.

Nip To go quickly, often with the implication of returning soon.

Abb. of nipple.

Nipper: A child or young adolescent.

Nish: Nothing.

Nit: A stupid person.

Nithered: Feeling very cold, frozen.

Nix: No, not, none.

Nobbing: An act of sexual intercourse. Also 'knobbing'.

Nobble: To tamper with, to damage. E.g."We were nobbled before the race began and came last."

Nobhead: An idiot, a contemptible person. Less common spelling of 'knobhead'.

Nob jockey: A homosexual male. Also 'knob jockey'.

Nob rot: Venereal disease.

Nodder: A condom.

Nod off: To fall asleep.

Noggin The head. E.g." Use your noggin, and think next time."

No mark: A nonentity, a person of no worth.

Noodle: 1. The head. E.g."For God's sake, use your noodle next time."

2. An idiot or imbecile.

Nookie: Sexual intercourse or it can simply be sexual activity in general. Considered fairly inoffensive. Also spelt *nooky*.

North: Mouth. Rhyming slang on *North and South.*

Nose-bag: Food or a meal. Derived from the method of feeding working horses via a bag of hay strung from its head and neck.

Nose blow: A handerkerchief or tissue for the purposes of wiping one's nose.

Nose candy: Cocaine.

Nose-rag: A handerkerchief.

Nose wipe: A handerkerchief or tissue for the purposes of wiping one's nose.

Nosey parker: An overly inquisitive person..

Nosh: Food.

1. To eat.

2. To fellate.

Noshery: An eating establishment, cafe, restaurant or snack bar. From 'nosh' (noun).

Nosh-up A good meal or feast.

Not all there: A euphemism for a little insane or eccentric.

Not give a toss: To not care at all.

Nous: Common-sense. E.g."If she had any nous, she wouldn't have stayed out until 5am getting drunk knowing she had a driving test at 10.30am."

Nowt: Nothing. E.g."There's nowt wrong with it, it works fine, honest!"

Nowty: Moody, angry.

Nuclear sub: A pub (public house), a bar. Rhyming slang.

Nugget: 1. A one pound coin (one pound sterling).

2. An idiot, fool.

Nuke: 1. To cook something on a very high heat and quickly.

2. To burn something during cooking.

Number: A cannabis or marijuana cigarette.

Number two(s): A euphemism for an act of defecation.

Numbnuts: An idiot.

Numero uno: 1. The best.

2. The top person, the most important person, the boss.

Numpty: A fool, idiot. Also spelt *numbty* and *numptie*.

Nut: To headbutt.

An insane or eccentric person.

Nutcase: A lunatic, an eccentric.

Nutjob: An idiot, crazy person.

Nutmeg: A skilful move in football (soccer) where a player with the ball gets past an opponent by kicking it between their legs.

To complete the action of the noun, nutmeg, above.

Nutter: Lunatic, idiot.

Nutty: Mad, eccentric or a little crazy.

O

Odd-fish: An eccentric or unusual person.

Offy: A shop that sells alcohol. An abbreviated form of *off licence.* Also spelt *offie.*

Oggin: 1. Sea.

2. Water.

Oik: An unsophisticated, uncultured and objectionable person.

Oily: A cigarette. From the rhyming slang 'oily rag', meaning 'fag'.

Old bag: An disagreeable, elderly woman.

Old banger: A delapidated old car.

Old bean: A form of address. E.g."Hello old bean, how are you today?"

Old boiler: 1. An unnattractive woman.

2. Wife.

Old boot: An objectionable, aging, unattractive woman.

Old chap: Affectionate term for one's penis.

Old cock:	Affectionate term of address for a man. Also 'old cocker'.
Old cocker:	A form of address, usually for a man. Occasionally shortened to 'cocker'.
Old fart:	An elderly, old fashioned and tedious person.
Old fellow:	Affectionate term for one's penis.
Old fruit:	A term of address.
Old hat:	Old fashioned.
Old lady:	Mother, girlfriend or wife.
Old man	1. Father, boyfriend or husband.
	2. Affectionate term for one's penis.
Once-over:	An inspection, a quick look over something or someone. E.g. "I was giving it the once over when the phone rang."
Oose:	Fluff.
Our kid:	1. One's younger brother or sister.
	2. Affectionate term for a friend.
Out:	Openly living as a homosexual.
Oxygen thief:	An elderly person.

P

Packed out:	Very crowded. E.g."The bar was so packed out, it took us 30 minutes to get served."
Packet:	1. The male genitals.
	2. A sizeable amount of money. E.g."I earnt a packet working overtime last weekend."
Pack up:	To break down. Usually said of a machine, however may on occasion be applied to ones bodyparts, such as, "my back's packed up."
	A snack, a packed lunch.
Pad:	One's apartment, room, home.
Paddy:	A rage, a tantrum or an upset. E.g "O.K., calm down, don't get in a paddy."
Paddy:	An Irish person. Derived from the popular and pet-form of the Irish name Padraig (Patrick). Often used offensively.

Paedo: Abb. of paedophile.

Pagga A fight. Also pagger.

To beat up, fight.

Paggered: Tired, exhausted.

Pain in the arse: Something or someone who is troublesome or tedious.

Pair: A euphemism for a woman's breasts.

Paki: 1. A Pakistani, but also used as a general and particularly offensive term for any pe on/immigrant from the Indian sub-continent, such as Pakistan, India, Bengal, Sri Lanka etc.

2. A shop or delicatessen run by asians.

Palatic: Drunk, intoxicated with alcohol. Also spelt pallatic and parlatic. Possibly a corruption of 'paralytic'.

Palaver: A tedious fuss or discussion. E.g."What's all this palaver about you and my mum having an argument?"

Pan handle: An erect penis. From the resemblance between the two.

Pansy: 1. An effeminate, feeble, weak-willed male.

2. A homosexual male.

Panto: Abb. of pantomine, being a theatrical show, mainly for children, and usually staged around the Christmas period.

Pap 1. Nonsense, rubbish.

2. Faeces.

To defecate. E.g."He was so scared he papped his pants."

Paps: Women's breasts.

Papers: Cigarette papers.

Para Paranoid.

Paraffin: A tramp, vagrant. Rhyming slang on paraffin lamp.

Paralytic: Extremely drunk.

Park one's arse: To sit down. E.g."Park your arse there a moment whilst I find my keys."

Parky: Cold, with regard to the weather.

Parp: 1. To break wind, to fart.

2. Nonsense, rubbish.

Party-pooper: Someone who is miserable and a spoilsport, consequently putting a damper on the pleasures of others.

Pash: An infatuation.

Passion killers: Very unattractive underwear and unlikely to encourage sexual advances; infact so unappealing they would halt any such advances.

Paste: To beat up.

Pasting: A beating. E.g. "He gave me a right pasting when he realised it was me that spread that rumour."

Pat and Mick: Affected with nausea, ill. Rhyming slang on sick. Also 'on the Pat and Mick'.

Paul Weller: Stella Artois, a popular brand of lager. Rhyming slang on Stella. Paul Weller, musician.

Pavement pizza: Vomit, when lying on the street.

P.d.q./ PDQ: Very quickly, immediately. Abb of Pretty Damned Quick. E.g."You best tidy up that mess p.d.q. Before your mother gets home."

Peahead: A person with a comparatively small head. Also pea head.

Peasouper: A very thick fog.

Peckish: Hungry. E.g."What time is dinner? I'm feeling a little peckish."

Pee: To urinate..

1. Urine.

2. An act of urination.

Pee it down: To rain heavily.

Peelie-wally: Pale looking, sickly.

Peeps: 1. Sleep.

2. People.

Peeve: Drink, usually alcoholic.

Peg-it: 1. To run, usually implying a sense or urgency, such as hurriedly.

2. To die.

Pen and ink: A stink, a bad smell. Cockney rhyming slang.

Pencil pusher: A person who works at a desk and whose job involves a large amount of paper-work or administration, such as a clerk.

Peng: 1. The best, great, excellent, often heard with reference to drugs. E.g."This weed is peng!"

2. Of a person, very attractive, desirable.

Percy: A pet name for the penis.

Perishing: 1. Used as an intensifier. E.g."That perishing dog was barking all night".

2. Very cold.. E.g."You should put your hat and scarf on, it's perishing outside."

Perve: Abb. of pervert.

To look lustfully or lecherously at someone or something. E.g."He shouldn't be allowed to work at the swimming pool, he's always perving over the ladies."

Pervy: Perverted.

Pet: A term of endearment.

Petal:	An affectionate term of address.
Petrolhead:	An enthusiast of cars and motoring, especially motor racing.
Phat:	1. Excellent, pleasing, desirable.
	2. Fashionable.
Phizog:	Face. Derived from physiognomy. Includes a number of variations in spelling phizzog, vissog, fizzog, physog, and phyzog.
Phwoah:	Used to express sexual desire at the sight of an attractive person. Imitative of the sound expressed in such a circumstance. Also spelt phwoar and phwoargh.
Pickled:	Drunk.
Piddle:	To urinate.
	1. Urine.
	2. An act of urination.
Piddle about:	To mess around, waste time.
Piddle it down	To rain.
Piddling:	Trivial, insignificant, small. E.g."I'm starving. You should have seen the piddling amount we had for dinner."
Piddly:	Small, trivial, insignificant.
Piece:	1. A euphemism for a gun.
	2. A female seen as a sexual object. A shortening of 'piece of skirt'.
	3. A sandwich.

Piece of cake: Something very easy. E.g."I got full marks in that quiz. It was a piece of cake."

Piece of shit: A contemptible person.

Pie-eater: 1. A simpleton.

2. A person from Wigan and surrounding area.

Pie-eyed: Drunk.

Piffle: Nonsense, drivel.

Piffling: Meaning the same as 'piddling'.

Pig-headed: Obstinate.

Pig-it: To act in an uncouth manner, to live below one's normal standards, to 'slob'.

Pig-ignorant: Very stupid, due to ignorance.

Pig-out: To eat fully and enthusiastically.

A big meal.

Pig's ear: 1. Beer. Cockney rhyming slang.

2. A mess, a disaster. E.g."I made a pig's ear of that job interview when I farted at the outset and couldn't stop giggling."

Pigshit: Rubbish, nonsense. E.g."You're talking a load of pigshit!"

Pikey: 1. A gypsy or traveller.

2. A vagrant.

Of or relating to a gypsy or vagrant.

Pilchard: An idiot.

Pill-head: A frequent abuser/user of illicit drugs in pill form, such as 'ecstasy' tablets.

Pillock: Idiot, fool. Originally a slang term for the penis but fairly inoffensive now its this meaning has been forgotten.

Pillow-biter: A homosexual male.

Pin A leg. Usually plural. E.g."That Brazilian model has got a fine pair of pins."

Pinch: 1. To steal. E.g."Guess who's just lost his job for pinching from work again?"

2. To arrest. E.g."He got pinched when he was climbing out of the kitchen window with the stolen TV."

Pinch a loaf: To defecate, to void one's bowels.

Pinhead: A person or creature with an unusually small head.

Pink cigar: The penis. Also in 'smoke a pink cigar'.

Pink oboe: The penis. Also in 'play the pink oboe'.

Pink pound: Disposable income that 'gays' ostensibly have through not having the financial expense of children.

Pint-sized: Small and compact.

Pip: To defeat by a small margin. Often heard in the expression 'pip at the post'. E.g."We pipped them to the finish and won by just 2 seconds."

Pipsqueek: A feeble, ineffectual person. .

Piss: To urinate.

1. Urine.

2. A weak drink.

An exclamation of anger, frustration.

Piss-arse: Insignificant, worthless.

Piss-artist: 1. A habitual drunk.

2. A contemptible time waster.

Piss-down To rain. E.g."It's pissing down outside, so take your brolly."

Piss easy: Very easy.

Pissed: Drunk.

Pissed off: Angry, upset or depressed.

Pissed up Very drunk.

Piss-flaps: The female genitals, particularly the labia.

An exclamation of annoyance.

Piss-head: A drunkard, a habitual drinker.

Pisshole: 1. A lavatory, a toilet.

2. An unpleasant, dirty place.

Piss it: To complete a task easily, to win effortlessly. E.g."They pissed it

	and won the trophy for the fourth year running."
Piss off:	1. To upset, to annoy. E.g."He had a reputation for pissing off the bar staff and getting thrown out of clubs."
	2. Go away. Heard frequently as an exclamation as piss off!
Piss oneself:	1. To laugh heartily. E.g."She pissed herself when I asked her out for a meal. Just because I'm 15 years younger than her."
	2. To be terrified.
Piss on:	To thoroughly defeat, or trounce. E.g."City pissed on United yesterday in their cup match."
Piss-poor:	Terrible, of low quality.
Piss-pot:	The toilet or toilet bowl. Orig referring to a chamber pot.
Piss-proud:	Having a penile erection on awaking in the morning; a common symptom due to one's bladder being full.
Piss-take:	A joke, a tease. Derived from the phrase 'take the piss'.
Piss-up	1. A drunken spree.
	2. A mess up, a bungled event.
Piss water:	Weak or tasteless drink, usually alcoholic.

Piss wet: Very wet, soaked.

Pissy: Weak, feeble, inferior. Often applied to drinks.

Pissy-arsed: Insignificant, inferior.

Pit: Bed. E.g."Oh, so you've finally got up out of your pit then? "

Pitch a tent: To have an erection whilst wearing clothing.

Pits: The worst imaginable situation, place or person.

Pit yakker: A coal miner.

Pizzaface: A person with bad spots, acne, or a generally very bad complexion.

Placky: Plastic.

Plank: An idiot.

Plastered: Drunk, intoxicated.

Plastic: Credit cards, cashpoint cards etc.

Synthetic, false.

Plate: To give oral sex, but more commonly to fellate.

Play around: To be sexually promiscuous.

Play it cool: To act calmly, to control ones emotions.

Pleb: An inferior, insignificant or common person. Abb. of plebeian.

Plebby: Common, ordinary.

Plod: A policeman/woman. From a character in Noddy, a series of children's books written by Enid Blyton in the 1950s.

Plod mag: A pornographic magazine.

Plonk: Cheap or inferior wine.

Plonker: 1. A penis.

2. Fool, idiot, a despicable person.

Plook: A spot, boil, 'zit'. Also spelt pluke.

Plop To defecate. Children's onomatopoeic euphemism.

Plug-ugly: Very ugly. Originally a ruffian, and taken from the New York gang of the mid 1800s, called the Plug Uglies.

Plums: Testicles.

Pocket rocket: Penis.

Podge: An overweight or obese person. Derived from the s.e. Podgy.

Pointies: A type of shoe with a pointed toe, usually women's.

Poison: Alcohol. Usually heard in questions such as "What's your poison?", meaning "What would you like to drink?"

Poison dwarf: An unpleasant, diminutive person.

Poke: To have sex with. A male expression.

Speed or power, usually applied to vehicles. E.g."His new car has plenty of poke."

Polish a turd: Heard in a negative context in the phrase you can't polish a turd, and when applied to a task means that it is impossible.

Poloney: A girl, young woman. Also polone and polony.

Polaxed: Drunk, intoxicated.

Pompey: The City of Portsmouth.

Ponce: 1. A contemptible person.

2. An effeminate male.

3. An ostentatious male.

Ponced up: Dressed up, overdressed.

The pond: The Atlantic Ocean.

Pond life: Person or persons of low intelligence, and not greatly evolved, as with creatures found in a pond.

Pong: An unpleasant smell.

To stink.

Poof: 1. A male homosexual. Also 'puff'.

2. A feeble, despicable person.

Pot: Marijuana.

Pot-head: An frequent user of marijuana or cannabis.

Potless: Poor, having no ready cash.

Potty: 1. Crazy, mad, eccentric.

2. Madly in love with, or mad about, something or someone. E.g."I was potty about Angelina Jolie for several years."

Pound: To have vigorous sex.

Pour it on To exaggerate. Also pour it on thick for added emphasis.

Povvy: Poor, something of poor class or low quality. From poverty.

Powfagged: Exhausted.

Poxy: 1. Rubbishy, crass, of poor quality.

2. A general negative intensifier. E.g."I'm not wasting my time and money by going to the poxy shops, just to keep her happy."

Pramface: A teenage mother, usually from a council housing estate. Coined by the online gossip site, Popbitch, and originally a woman with the facial looks of a poor single mother as seen around a housing estate.

Prannet: An idiot, an imbecile, or objectionable person. Possibly derived from 'pranny'.

Prannock: An idiot. A variation of 'prannet'.

Pranny: An idiot, a fool. Originally a male term of contempt meaning the female genitals.

Prat: A fool, idiot or objectionable person. Originally meaning the buttocks.

Preggars: Pregnant. A corruption of the word pregnant.

Pretty-boy: An attractive young man, pretty as opposed to handsome or manly.

Previous: A criminal record. Usually police and criminal vernacular. E.g."Be careful if you decide to employ him, he has some previous."

Prezzie: A present, a gift. Also *pressie.*

Prick: 1. The penis.

2. An idiot, contemptible person.

Prick-teaser: Someone who knowingly exploits the fact that they are sexually alluring.

Private parts: The genitals. Often shortened to privates.

Pro Abb. of prostitute.

Proper: Used as an intensifier. E.g." I think the cat has crapped under the bed, as there's a proper stink in the bedroom."

Prozzy: A corruption of the word prostitute.

Pudding: 1. An uncomplimentary but jocular and affectionate name for someone who is plump.

2. A term of endearment.

Puddle: A mess, a confused state. E.g."Sorry, i've been in a bit of puddle since the party. I drank far too much."

Puff: 1. A male homosexual. Also poof and pouf.

2. A feeble, despicable person.

Puggled: Crazy, mad.

Puke: To vomit. E.g."He drank so much at his stag party he spent the next 2 days puking up."

Vomit.

Pukka Excellent, wonderful. Derived from the s.e. Use of pukka, meaning genuine, and in itself derived from the Hindi pakka, meaning thorough or substantial.

Pull a job: To commit a robbery. E.g."I pulled a job at the local post office so I'm lying low for a few days."

Pull a pig: To seduce an ugly person. Also a cruel game of the same name, played by friends on a night out, the object being to seduce the ugliest person.

Pull one's pud: Of males, to masturbate. E.g."Pulling your pud all night is hardly what you mother had in mind when she said do something creative."

Pump To break wind, to 'fart'. E.g."I'm not sitting next to Louise, she's always pumping and I can't concentrate on my work."

Pumping: Lively, energetic, thrilling. E.g."What was that last tune the DJ played? It was pumpin'."

Punaani: Female genitals.

Punch up: A fist fight, a brawl.

Punkette: A female 'punk'

Punter: Generally a customer of any business.

Puppies: Female breasts.

Put it about: Have frequent sexual liasons with numerous partners.

Putzy: Easy, simple. Also putsy.

Q

Queen	A male homosexual, particularly one who is effeminate.
Queer:	A homosexual. Once, only derogative, but now the expression is being reclaimed by the gay community.
	Homosexual in nature.
Queer bashing:	Prejudicial aggression or intimidation toward homosexuals.
Quickie:	A brief sexual liason. E.g."I'm off home for my lunch break, for a quickie with the wife, it beats eating in the company cafeteria."
Quid:	One pound sterling.
Quids-in	In profit. E.g."After the deduction of my expenses I was still quids-in."
Quim	The vagina or more generally the female genitals. Possibly from the Celtic cwm, a valley.

R

Rack:	The female breasts, usually when impressively large.
Rad:	Excellent, wonderful. Often an exclamation of approval. Possibly from radical.
Radgie:	Crazy. Also radgey.
Rag head:	An arab, Sikh, or other race or religion that traditionally wears cloth headwear.
Raging:	Great, immense, extreme. A general intensifier. E.g."I had a raging headache last night".
Rags:	Clothes.
Rag trade:	The garment industry.
Rag week:	The period of menstruation, usually with negative connotations of moodyness.
Rainbow kiss:	Cunnilingus when performed on a menstruating woman.
Rain stair rods:	To rain very heavily.
Ralph:	To vomit.

Rammy: Vile, unsavoury, rotten.

Ram-raid: The use of a vehicle to smash into a property so as to steal the goods, usually a shop.

Random: Cool, excellent, great.

Rare: Good, excellent. E.g."We had a rare time at the party last night. The best for a long time."

Rat-arsed: Very drunk.

Rat on To inform on, betray.

Ratty: Irritable.

Raving: The act of going to a 'rave'.

Ravey: In the manner of a 'rave'.

Reefer: A marijuana or cannabis cigarette. Dated and rarely used seriously.

Reet: Alright, correct, OK. Basically a mispronounciation of right.

Rellies: Relatives. E.g."I'm afraid we can't come over this evening, Zoe's rellies are visiting."

Rent-boy: A male prostitute.

Retard: A contemptible person. A term usually used by adolescents.

Riah: Hair. Backslang originating from Polari, consequently heard mainly on the Gay scene.

Rib: To tease, make fun of.

Rice queen: A gay male who prefers asian partners.

Ricker:	The anus.
Rifle range:	Loose change. Rhyming slang.
Right:	Used as an intensive. E.g."I made a right mess of that." E.g."I'm right glad to hear that you two are friends again."
Rim	To stimulate a persons anus with the tongue for sexual pleasure.
Rim job:	The act of using one's tongue to stimulate a persons anus, for sexual pleasure.
Ringer:	1. A second hand car made to appear in much better quality than it is. 2. A person with high skills brought into a sports team for a game or competition.
Ring-sting:	Soreness of the anus, due to diarrhoea.
Ring-stinger:	A hot and spicy curry. One, that on digestion, may cause looseness of the bowels and diarrhoea.
Ringtum:	The anus.
Rinse:	1. To overdo, overplay. E.g."It may be a classic but that tune's been rinsed, play something new will you?" 2. As *rinse it*, to go for it, to enjoy, to party.

Rip-off: To con, to swindle.

1. A contrick, a act of deception.

2. An illicit copy. E.g."Dont buy any computer software from that market stall, it's all ripped off."

Roaring: A general intensifier, extremely, very. Often heard in the phrase *roaring drunk*.

Rock: Freebased cocaine, 'crack'. From its physical appearence.

Rogering: An act of sexual intercourse.

Roll-up To make a cigarette by hand.

A handrolled cigarette.

Rollick: To reprimand, chastise. Often heard pronounced as rollock.

Rollie: A handrolled cigarette.

Root: To have sexual intercourse.

Rot: Nonsense. E.g."Don't talk rot! What you've just said is total nonsense."

Rouf: The number four. Backslang. Often representing 4-1 odds in tic-tac betting slang.

Rough: A person for a bit of easy sex but below one's usual standard.

Rough-it: To live without all the usual pleasures and amenities.

Row: 1. A noisy quarrel.

2. A loud noise.

Rub-a-dub: A public house. Rhyming slang, on pub.

Rubber cheque: A monetary cheque (check) that isn't honoured by the writer's bank, consequently bouncing back to the issuer.

Rubbered: Drunk, intoxicated.

Rub-off: To sexually excite by manual stimulation of the genitals.

Rub-up: Meaning the same as 'rub-off'.

Rude girl: Female version of 'rude boy'.

Rude bits: A euphemism for the genitals. E.g."Getting a cricket ball in the rude bits is seriously painful."

Rug: A wig.

Rug muncher: A lesbian.

Rug rat: A young child.

Ruined: Drunk, intoxicated with alcohol.

Rum: Strange, odd, peculiar. E.g."That new kid's a bit rum, he's always talking to himself."

Rumble: To discover, to find out. E.g."She rumbled me when she overheard my conversation on the phone."

Rum go: A surprising event.

Rumpy-pumpy: Sexual intercourse. Jocular use.

Runs: To have diarrhoea.

Runt: A despicable person.

Rush: 1. A surge of pleasurable feelings from taking drugs.

2. The surging onset of the effects of a drug, occasionally including queasiness.

Rust bucket: A dilapidated rusty old car, or vehicle.

S

Sack: 1. Bed. E.g."Let's hit the sack, I'm exhausted."

2. Dismissal from employment.

Sack-it: Stop it, put an end to something.

Sad: 1. Unfortunate, pitiful or pathetic. E.g."Geoff's so sad, getting his tongue pierced just because it's fashionable."

2. Objectionable.

Sad arse: 1. A pathetic person.

2. General insult for someone who acts contemptuously.

Saddo A pathetic or contemptible person.

Sad sack: A miserable, pathetic person.

Saft: Stupid, soft.

Salad dodger: A fat person.

Sand grown: A person born in one of the West Lancs coastal towns, e.g. Blackpool, Morecombe etc. Also a sand grown 'un.

Sand niggar: An Arab, or more widely a person from the Middle East.

Sandwich: A sexual threesome.

Sapphic: Of or like a lesbian.

Sanger: A sandwich.

Sarky: Abb. of sarcastic.

Sarnie: A sandwich.

Sauce: Alcoholic drink. E.g."He's going to feel bad in the morning, after 12 hours on the sauce."

Sausage: A penis.

Sausage jockey: A homosexual male.

Savvy: In the know, well informed.

S.B.D. A silent breaking of wind that is particularly foul smelling. Abb. of Silent But Deadly.

Scabby: Unpleasant, distasteful, rotten.

Scam A trick or con.

Scanties: Female underwear. From their often exiguous nature.

Scaredy-cat: A person who is frightened. Mainly adolescent use, often employed as a taunt.

Scatty: Absent-minded. Possibly from scatterbrained.

Scav: Abb of scavenger.

To scavenge.

Schemie:	A disparaging term for a person from a Scottish council estate, called a scheme.
Schlep	To tiresomely lug around, to do lots of leg work. Also spelt 'shlepp'. The term gained popularity in Britain during the late 1980s.
Schlong:	Penis. Also spelt shlong.
Schmooze:	To chat intimately and in a flattering manner.
Schpiel:	Persuasive talk.
Scoff:	To eat.
	Food.
Sconner:	A person without pubic hair.
Scouse:	Of, or, from Liverpool. Derived from the name of a local stew, an abb. of lobscouse.
Scrag:	1. To throttle, strangle.
	2. To handle roughly.
Scran	Food.
Scrap	A fight or quarrel.
Scratcher:	Bed.
Scratter:	1. A slovenly dressed person, a dirty person, perhaps of low intelligence and having little culture.
	2. A contemptible person.

Screw: 1. To copulate. E.g."Yeah I think they like each other, they screwed all night and kept us awake with their noise."

2. To cheat, to swindle.

Screw up To ruin, mess up. E.g."Don't screw up your life with jugs! No sorry, I meant drugs."

A failure, a 'cock-up'.

Scrikey: Tearful.

Scrote: 1. A contemptible person.

2. An abb. of scrotum.

3. A young criminal.

Scrotty: Unpleasant, dirty.

Scrubber: A coarse and sexually amenable or promiscuous woman.

Scruff: An unkempt or dirty person.

Scrummy: Delicious, pleasant, occasionally sexually appealing. Derived from the informal *scrumptious.*

Scrump: To steal fruit from a garden or orchard.

Scuffer: A policeman.

Scum A worthless person or persons.

Scumbag: 1. A despicable or objectionable person.

2. A sleazy person.

Scumbucket: Meaning the same as 'scumbag'.

Scunt: A contemptible person.

Scupper: To thwart, to prevent from succeeding. E.g."Don't scupper your chances of passing your driving test by having a beer first."

Scut: A sexually promiscuous woman.

Scutch: Sting or smart from a slap.

Scuzzy: Filthy, dirty, unkempt.

Semi: A half erect penis; abb. of semi-erection.

Senga A young, poorly educated female who wears casual sportswear and is of working class upbringing. The female equivalent of a 'ned'.

Set of wheels: A vehicle or a wheeled means of transport.

Sex on a stick: A sexually attractive, slim, woman.

Sex on legs: A sexually desirable person, usually applied to women.

Sex wee: Ejaculate, semen.

Shade: Unfair, questionable, disreputable, dubious. Probably from *shady*.

Shaft: 1. To fornicate. Male terminology.

2. To con, treat unfairly.

Shag: To copulate, to have sex. Less coarse than 'fuck'. E.g."The first night we met we shagged all night."

Shagbag: A sexually amenable or available woman.

Shaggable: Sexually desirable. Also *shagable.*

Shagged: Worn out, exhausted. Also often combined with *out* or *up*. E.g."I'm shagged out after my 26 mile run."

Shagging: Sexual intercourse.

Shag out: To wear out, to tire out. E.g."He shagged out the engine by forgetting to top up the oil."

Shagtastic: 1. Sexually desirable, sexy.

2. Excellent, wonderful, by extension of meaning 1. E.g."It was a shagtastic Ferrari."

Shambolic: In a mess, disorganised, mismanaged.

Shan: Unfair.

Shanks's pony: On foot, walking. E.g."Looks like we've missed the bus, so it's Shanks's pony or wait another hour for the next bus."

Shant: A drink, usually alcohol.

Sharpish: Quickly. E.g."You had better hurry to shops pretty damned sharpish, before they close"

Shat: To have defecated, the past tense of 'shit'. E.g."I shat my pants when I saw the size of him, he was very scary."

Shattered: Worn out, exhausted.

Shaven haven: A depilated pubic region, usually of women, and viewed as sexually desirable.

Sheet: Paper money, monetary notes. E.g."My new computer cost me 800 sheets."

Shell out: To pay up, to hand over, usually money. E.g."I shelled out over £1000 for that holiday."

Sherman: An act of masturbation. Cockney rhyming slang. Sherman tank, rhyming with 'wank'.

Sheila A woman. Stereotypical but jocular use when impersonating Australians and their vernacular.

Shift oneself: A request to move oneself. Used in imper. E.g."Will you shift yourself so I can vacuum the lounge."

Shift one's arse: To move out of the way or to hurry up. E.g."Come on, shift your arse and help me tidy up, my parents will be here soon."

Shirtlifter: A homosexual male.

Shirty: Ill-tempered. E.g."Pete got all shirty with me when I didn't invite him for dinner."

Shit: 1. Faeces.

2. An act of defecation.

Shitbag:	A contemptible person.
Shitbox:	1. The anus.
	2. A contemptible thing, place or person.
Shit eater:	A contemptible person. Also shiteater.
Shitehawk:	1. A despicable person.
	2. A seagull.
Shitepipe:	The anus.
Shiter:	The anus. A variation on 'shitter'.
Shit-face:	A contemptible person.
Shit-faced:	1 Drunk, intoxicated.
	2. Intoxicated with drugs.
Shit for brains:	A particularly stupid person, a contemptible person.
Shit-head:	An contemptible person.
Shit-hot:	Excellent, the best, extremely good.
Shitless:	Very frightened. Usually preceded by the word bored or scared.
Shitloads:	A large amount.
Shits:	Diarrhoea. E.g."I can't come out tonight, i've got the shits."
Shit-stabber:	A homosexual male.
Shitstain	A contemptible person.
Shit stirrer:	An insidious gossip, a person whose malicious actions cause problems for others.

Shit stirring: Trouble making, for the sake of it.

Shit stoppers: 1. Very narrow, tight fitting jeans.

2. Tracksuit bottoms with elasticated ankles.

Shitter: 1. The anus.

2. A toilet.

3. A contemptible person.

Shit-tip: A mess. E.g."Tommy, you're not going to Macdonalds until you tidy your bedroom, it's a bloody shit-tip!"

Shonky: Dubious, unreliable, underhand.

Shoot blanks: Of a man, to be sterile. Also phrased as fire blanks.

Shoot off: To leave quickly, to hurriedly go. E.g."I'm just going to shoot off down to the post office before it closes."

Shoot-up To inject a drug.

Shop To tell or inform on.

Shopping: 1. A euphemism for illicit drugs as brought from a drug dealer.

2. Shoplifting.

Short-arse: A person who is small in stature.

Shot: Worn out, exhausted..

Shotgun: A way of smoking cannabis/ marijuana between two people, with one person blowing and the other inhaling.

Shout: A round of drinks. E.g."Go on, get to the bar you lazy sod, it's your shout."

Shower: A derogatory and all encompassing term for a motley group of people.

Shrammed: Cold, frozen. Also occasionally numbed by extension of being frozen.

Shrapnel: Money in the form of loose change.

Shreddies: Underwear.

Shufflebutt: A fidgety, restless person.

Shushy: A 'camp', extravagant style. Many spelling alternatives including zhoosy, jujjy, zuzshy.

Sickie: A period away from work with illness, and usually without just medical cause.

Sicko A disturbing and unsavoury person, a pervert.

Silly sausage: A foolish person.

Sissy: An effeminate, weak, or cowardly person.

Sitter: In sport, an easy catch or shot, that should result in points being scored.

Six-pack: Strong and evident abdominal muscles.

Size queen A gay male with a sexual preference for partners with large genitalia.

Skag: Heroin. Also spelt 'scag'.

Skanger: A young, working class person who dresses in casual sportswear.

Skank: To steal, thieve. E.g."Someone's skanked my cigarettes and it was nearly a full packet!"

Skanky: Dirty, unnattractive, ugly, smelly.

Skanky pants: Dirty, or disgusting, lingerie or underwear. Also occasionally skanky panties, but this is more U.S.

Skedaddle: Move, go away.

Skeg: A look at. E.g."Give us a skeg at your paper, I need to check the racing results."

Skelf: A splinter.

Skew-whiff: Out of alignment, incorrect.

Skid lid: A motorcycle helmet.

Skidmark: A faecal smear or stain. Usually with regard to one's undergarments.

Skids: 1. Underwear, underpants, knickers.

2. Excrement smears or stains, usually with respect to one's underpants. Abb. of 'skidmark'.

Skin diver: A five pound (sterling) note. Rhyming slang on 'fiver'.

Skin flute: The penis.

Skinful: A sufficient quantity of alcohol to make one drunk. E.g."I'm not driving anywhere; i've had a skinful and the police are out in force."

Skinny: Information, details. E.g."What's the skinny with that new man in accounts?"

Skins: Cigarette papers, but refers more to those used in a 'joint.'

Skint: Having no money, poor.

Skin up To roll or build a cannabis/ marijuana cigarette. E.g."Anyone who was spotted skinning up was arrested and given a police warning."

Skirt: A woman or women.

Skit: To make fun of, to tease.

Skitters: A bout of diarrhoea. E.g."I'm not coming into work today, i've got the skitters."

Skive: An evasion of one's tasks, a period of shirking.

Skiver: A shirker, one who evades doing their work or duties.

Skivvy: A servant for menial tasks.

Skunkweed: A type of very strong marijuana.

Skypilot: A priest, vicar or similar preacher of religion.

Slap Cosmetic make-up. Originally from theatrical usage.

To beat-up, hit, thump. E.g."I'm going to slap that bastard if he doesn't shut up."

Slaphead: A balding person.

Slapper: 1. A sexually promiscuous woman.

2. A contemptible woman.

Slappy: A pie sandwich. Usually a meat pie on a bread bun.

Slap-up To apply cosmetic make-up.

Extravagent and sumptuous. Usually applied to meals or dinner. E.g."It's my birthday so we're off out for a slap-up meal, and I'm paying!"

Slash: To urinate. Onomatopoeic.

An act of urination.

Slaughtered: 1. Very intoxicated by drink or drugs.

2. Exhausted, worn out.

Sleazebag: A despicable, sleazy, fawning person.

Sleazeball: Meaning the same as 'sleazebag'.

Sledge:	To be incapacitated mentally, and consequently physically, from taking drugs. E.g."I just sat there sledging in the corner, unable to dance."
Slimeball:	A repugnant person. Also shortened to slime.
Slit:	The vagina.
Slob:	A uncouth, unsavoury and lazy person.
Slo-mo	Slowly. Abb. of slow-motion.
Sloshed:	Drunk.
Slot:	Hurt, injure, stab, shoot. E.g."I slotted that bastard last year, and he spent 3 weeks in hospital."
Slum-it:	To live without the usual pleasures.
Slummock:	A dirty, untidy or lazy person.
	To behave in a lazy and unkempt fashion.
Slummy:	Loose change.
Slutty:	Sluttish.
Smack:	Heroin. Derived from the Yiddish schmeck.
Smacker:	1. A loud kiss. From the noise it might make.
	2. One pound sterling, although usually in the plural. E.g."She still owes me 40 smackers from last week."

Smackeroos: Meaning the same as 'smacker', but with a more lighthearted slant. E.g."I can't wait to get my hands on all those lovely smackeroos when I collect my winnings."

Smackhead: A heroin addict, junkie.

Smackie: Heroin addict. From 'smack', meaning heroin. E.g."If I was you I wouldnt go in the park after dark, it's usually full of smackies."

Smarmy: Obsequious, condescendingly flattering.

Smart-arse: A person who smuggly displays their intelligence.

Smart-arsed: Smuggly displaying ones cleverness.

Smarty-pants: A know-all. Also smartie-pants.

Smashed: Very intoxicated with drink or drugs.

Smashing: Excellent, brilliant, wonderful. E.g."We had a smashing time at the circus."

Smashingly: Very well, without any problems. E.g."Yes we had a great time, the holiday went smashingly."

Smeg: Abb. of smegma.

An exclamation of annoyance.

Smeggy: Unsavoury, horrible. The word derives from smegma.

Smeghead:	An idiot, an objectionable person. Popularized on Red Dwarf, a British sit-com, for the humorous usage. Also smeg head.
Smellies:	Scented toiletries and perfumes.
Smelly:	A biker, usually unkempt, long haired, and a listener of rock music.
Smelly-bridge:	The perineum. From the area bridging one smelly place to another (the genitals to the anus).
Smidge:	A little, a small amount. An abbreviated form of 'smidgeon'.
Smidgeon	A little, a small amount.
Smoothie:	A person who is over stylish and suave.
SNAFU:	A bad situation, a mistake, a foul-up. Acronym of situation normal all fucked up.
Snail-mail:	Post, surface mail. Jocular expression coined with the advent of the speedier and generally immediate email.
Snap:	Food, especially a snack, occasionally a packed lunch.
Snappin:	Food.
Snatch:	The female genitals.
Snazzy:	Smart or attractive in an ostentatious way.
Sneep:	To insult, to upset. Also sneap.

Sneeped: Hurt, offended.

Snitcher: An informer.

Snockered: Drunk, intoxicated.

Snook-cocking: Showing contempt. From 'cock a snook'.

Snookered: Defeated, thwarted.

Snot rag: A handkerchief.

Snurge: A person who smells bicycle seats for sexual pleasure.

Soak: A drunkard.

So-and-so A contemptible person. Mildy offensive.

Soap-dodger: An unkempt, dirty person.

Softy: A weak, feeble or overly sentimental person.

Soopy: A supermarket. Unknown spellings, perhaps also supie or supey.

Sort: An attractive woman.

Sound: O.K., wonderful, similar to 'sorted.'

Sounds: Tunes or music. E.g."Have you brought any new sounds for tonight's party."

Sovs: Money. Abb. of sovereign, £1 sterling.

Soz: Sorry. Mainly adolescent use.

Sozzled: Drunk, but not incapacitated.

Spac:	An imbecile, objectionable person. From spastic. Offens.
Spacey:	Ambient, ethereal.
Spacky:	Idiotic, stupid. Also spaccy. From spac. Offens.
Spadger:	A sparrow.
Spaff:	Semen.
Spam fritter:	The anus. Rhyming slang on 'shitter'.
Spangled:	Very intoxicated by alcohol or drugs.
Spaniel's ears:	Saggy, flat, droopy breasts. From their similarity.
Spanner:	An idiot, a contemptible person.
Spare-tyre:	A roll of fat around one's midrift.
Spark:	An electrician.
Spark out:	To pass out, become unconscious.
Spark up	To light a cigarette, and often with regards to a 'joint'.
Spatchcock:	To add a phrase, clause or sentence in a context that is inappropriate.
Spawny:	Lucky.
Spazmo:	Imbecile, objectionable person. Derived from spastic. Offens.
Spazmobile:	1. A car for the disabled. 2. An objectionable, unstylish car.

Spazzy: Stupid,

2. Uncool, not fashionable.

Special K: The drug ketamine.

Speed: The drug amphetamine sulphate.

Speed freak: 1. A compulsive user, or addict, of amphetamines.

2. A person who loves driving fast.

Speeding: Under the influence of amphetamine sulphate.

Speg: Chewing gum.

Spell: A splinter.

Spends: Money to spend on oneself, often with respect to children's pocket money.

Spesh: Abbreviated form of special. E.g."Last night was really spesh!"

Spew: Vomit.

To vomit.

Spew-up To vomit.

Spice: Confectionery.

Spidge: Chewing gum.

Spinny: Strange, unusual, confusing. E.g."That new kid's spinny, and I dont trust him."

Spiggy: Chewing gum. Cf 'spoggy'.

Spit: An exact double, an identical image.

Spit tacks: Be very angry. E.g."She was spitting tacks after I stained her best table cloth with ketchup."

Splick: Distasteful or unpleasant viscous substances.

Spliff: A cannabis or marijuana cigarette.

Split arse: A woman.

Split beaver: An explicit pornographic pose fully revealing the female genitals.

Splosh: Tea (the drink).

Spoof: Semen.

Spraff: To chat, talk. E.g."Don't just stand there spraffing, find some work to do."

Spreathed: Sore through exposure to cold weather, chapped.

Sprog: A child.

Sprogged up: Pregnant. From 'sprog' meaning child.

Spud ugly: Very ugly.

Squaddie: A soldier.

Square: A person who is reactionary, old fashioned and set in their ways.

Square-eyes: A humourous address for someone who watches too much television.

Square-go: A fist fight, a punch up.

Squicky: Disgusting.

Squid: A jocular term for one pound sterling, derived from 'quid'.

Squillion A very large indefinite amount.

Squinny: One who moans or complains.

Squire: A term of address.

Squirt: A diminutive and insignificant person.

Squiz: A look, a glance. E.g."Have a squiz at the photos and see if you can spot anyone you recognise."

Stacked: Of a woman, well built or large breasted.

Stalk: An erect penis.

Stiff: 1. A dead body.

2. A boring conventional person.

Stinker: 1. A contemptible person.

2. An awkward, difficult task.

Stitch up To betray with false evidence. Also phrased to stitch someone up.

Stoater: Something impressive or excellent.

Stocious: Intoxicated.

Stomp on: To physically assault.

Stomping: Lively, energetic. E.g."That last tune the DJ played was stomping."

Stone bonker: A sure thing, a certainty.

Stonker: 1. An erect penis, usually implying great size.

2. Something huge or impressive.

Stoppy back: An after hours drink at a public house.

Storming: Marvellous, excellent. E.g."We had a storming night out at the club, the best ever."

Stottie: A flat coarse bread, made from the scraps of dough leftover in baking.

Stowed out: Crowded, packed out, full to capacity.

Straight: 1. A heterosexual.

2. A conventional but boring person.

Strap-on A substitute penis that can be worn by females to simulate male to female sexual intercourse.

Strap up: To make a cannabis/marijuana cigarette.

Stretch: A period spent in prison.

Strides: Trousers:

Stringbean A tall, thin person..

Stroppy: Bad tempered.

Strum: An act of female masturbation.

Stuck-up Conceited, snobbish.

Studmuffin: An attractive male.

Stump up To pay up, to hand over what is owed.

Suck off: To give oral sex (to someone). E.g."I lay down on the sofa so she could suck me off."

Suck up To flatter, be obsequious.

Suit: A white-collar worker, a business executive.

Sunshine: A form of address. E.g."Alright sunshine! Show us what you've got."

Sup To drink. E.g."It's no wonder you've got a headache, you've been supping beer all day."

Suss: Abb. of suspicious. E.g."I don't like the looks of that bloke, he's suss."

Sussed: Knowledgeable, well-informed, able to look after oneself.

Swap spit: To kiss deeply.

Sweet: Excellent, a general term of approval.

Sweet-pea: A term of affection.

Swimbo: Acronym. One's wife or girlfriend. Standing for She Who Must Be Obeyed.

Swinger: A person who indulges in partner swapping for sexual variety.

Swirly: The act of forcing a victim's head down a toilet bowl whilst simultaneously flushing it. Also occasionally swirlie.

Swizz: A swindle.

Swot: A person who studies hard.

To study hard. E.g."Timmy had been swotting for 3 months, but still failed his exams."

Swotty: Studious.

Swot up: To study hard.

Syrup: A wig. Abb. of the rhyming slang Syrup of Fig; making a comeback into everyday usage.

T

Tab:	1. Abb. of tablet. Drug culture expression. 2. A cigarette.
Tab-end:	A cigarette butt.
Table-ender:	An act of copulation on or at a table.
Tacky:	Of poor taste, lacking style.
Tadger:	A penis. Usually affectionate usage.
Tag:	A pseudonym or other identifying mark used as a signature by a graffitti artist.
Tagnuts:	Faecal remnants that adhere to anal hairs.
Tailor-made:	A factory produced cigarette, as opposed to a hand-rolled cigarette.
Taint:	The perineum. Something of a pun, because it aint the anus, and it aint the vagina or balls.
Take a dive:	To feign a foul or knockdown in sports.

Take a hike: To depart. Usually a demand by someone.

Take it easy: 1. Goodbye, a parting salutation.

2. Relax, don't get stressed.

Take five: Have a brief rest or respite from one's current activities.

Talent: An attractive person or persons.

Tallywhacker: Penis.

Tap off: To seduce a sexually desirable person.

Tart up To smarten up.

Tash: Abb. of moustache.

Tasty: Attractive.

Tat: 1. Rubbish, junk. Abb. of tatty. E.g."You can't wear that old cardigan, it's tat."

2. Abb. of tattoo.

Taters: Potatoes. A corruption of the word potatoes.

Tealeaf: Thief. Cockney rhyming slang.

Tear-jerker: A film or story likely to be over sentimental and promote tearful emotions.

Techno A type of electronically created dance music.

Teenth: Drug parlance for a sixteenth of an ounce.

Telly: Television.

Tenner: A ten-pound (sterling) monetary note.

Tex mex: Marijuana.

Thang: Thing.

Thatch: Pubic hair.

Thicko An stupid, unintelligent person.

Thrash: A type of fast raw rock music derived from 'punk'.

Threads: Clothes.

Threesome: An act of sex between three people, a menage a trois.

Throat yogurt: Semen. Also spelt throat yoghurt.

Throne: The lavatory, the toilet.

Throw: 1. To vomit. A shortening of 'throw up'.

2. To intentionally or by one's own foolishness, lose a game.

Throw up To vomit.

Tickled pink: Very pleased.

Tick off: To reprimand, to tell off. E.g."If you keep ticking me off then i'll go home early and then you'll be sorry."

Ticked off: Angry, annoyed.

Tickety-boo Fine, all right, in order. E.g."Yes indeed, everything is just tickety-boo, i've never felt better."

Tiddly: 1. A little drunk.

2. Small.

Tidy: Good, satisfactory. Common use in Wales. E.g."It was a tidy party, but i've got a terrible hangover now."

Tight: 1. To be frugal or not generous.

2. Drunk.

Tight-arse: A mean, selfishly frugal person.

Tight-arsed: Mean, stingy.

Tightwad: A miserly person, a mean person.

Time: A prison sentence. *Serving one's time*, or *doing time.*

Tinkle: 1. An act of urination. Much accepted expression, less vulgar than 'widdle.'

2. A phone-call. E.g."I'll give you a tinkle at the weekend.".

Tinnie: A can of beer.

Tip A style, manner. E.g."That tune was very much on an operatic tip."

Tip it down To rain heavily. E.g."It's been tipping it down for 40 days and nights."

Tip off: To give information secretly.

An act of revealing secret information.

Tit boring: Very boring, tedious.

Titch: A nickname for a small person.

Titchy: Tiny, small, insignificant.

Titfer: A hat. Cockney rhyming slang from *tit for tat.*

Tit-head: An idiot, a despicable person.

Tizzy: A confused, flustered state. E.g."She was all emotional and in a tizzy.".

Todger: A penis. A variation on 'tadger'.

To do A fuss, a fracas..

Toe-jam The dirt that collects between one's toes.

Toe-job: An act of licking/sucking a person's toes, usually for sexual gratification.

Toff: A member of the wealthy upper classes.

Toffee-nosed: Snobbish.

Togger: Football. Generally adolescent/ juvenile use.

Togs: Clothes.

Toke: To smoke a 'joint', or marijuana cigarette.

A drag on a cigarette or 'joint'.

Toley: A lump of excrement. Also spelt toly and tolli.

Tommies: Tomatoes.

Tomtit: An act of defecation. From the rhyming slang for 'shit'.

Ton The figure of one hundred, usually applied to the speed of 100 mph or a sum of £100.

Tongue: To perform cunnilingus.

Tonky: A condom.

Tonsil hockey: Passionate, deep kissing.

Tonsil tennis: Passionate, deep kissing.

Tool: 1. A penis, implying its supposed usefulness.

2. An idiot, a contemptible person.

Tool-up To arm oneself, usually with a gun.

Tooled up Armed, carrying weapons.

Toot: Originally to snort drugs but now also smoking.

Tootsies: Toes.

Top dog: The leader, boss.

Top one: Excellent, expressing that something is the best.

Topper: An exceptional thing or person. Dated expression.

Top totty: Very attractive woman, or women.

Torch: To set alight.

Tossbag: A contemptible or worthless person.

Tosser: An idiot, a contemptible person. Also, occasionally spelt tossa.

Toss-pot: Mildly offensive name for an idiot or contemptible person. Often heard used affectionately.

Totty: Sexually alluring female or females, also applied, these days, to males. Originally a term for a prostitute in late 1800s. E.g."There was plenty of totty at the party."

Tough guy: A particularly hard and unyielding male, scared of little and acting so.

Tough nut: A difficult or obstinate person.

Toyboy: A woman's evidently younger male lover.

Tracky: Tracksuit. E.g."Can I borrow your tracky bottoms? Mine are in the wash."

Tramlines: The scars created by the constant injection of illicit drugs.

Tranks: Tranquillizers.

Trap off: To attain a liason with a sexually desirable person. Also just phrased as trap.

Trap The mouth. E.g."Shut your trap you noisy bugger."

Treacle: An affectionate term of address, more prevalent in London.

Treader: A bicycle.

Tree hugger: An environmentalist, a green activist.

Trick cyclist: A pun on psychiatrist.

Triffid: Any large or sprawling plant, usually a house plant. From The Day of the Triffids by John Wyndham.

Triphop	Variety of dance music that draws its influences from 'hip-hop' and 'house', but being deeper and a little more orientated towards listening.
Trippy:	Of or like the experiences and qualities felt under the influence of hallucinogens.
Trog:	An ugly, uncouth person. Derived from troglodyte.
Troll:	An ugly person, usually referring to a woman.
Tromp	To trudge, to walk. E.g."I'm worn out, having tromped around the shops for the last 6 hours."
Trough:	To eat. The imagery is of eating like an animal.
Trousered:	Drunk, or very intoxicated.
Trousers:	Nonsense, gibberish.
Trouser snake:	Euphemism for the penis. A shortening of 'one-eyed trouser-snake'.
Trouser tent:	A penile erection, when visible beneath clothing.
Trout:	An unattractive woman, often prefixed with old.
Tubby:	A fat person, often of short stature.
Tube:	A contemptible or idiotic person.
Tub of lard:	A fat person.

Tuck: Food.

Tuck shop: A confectioners, a sweet shop. Children's expression.

Tug: An act of male masturbation.

Turd fish: A lump of faecal excrement, when viewed floating in water.

Turf: The area felt to belong to a person or gang.

Turkey: A stupid or idiotic person.

Turnip: 1. An idiot.

2. The head.

Turn-off: To disgust.

A thing that is disgusting.

Turn-on To excite, often sexually.

Something that excites.

Turn over: To rob by ransacking a premises. E.g."The library got turned over at the weekend and three computers got stolen."

Twannock: An idiot, an objectionable person.

Twat: 1. The female genitals.

2. A contemptible person, an idiot.

Twerp An imbecile, a fool. Fairly inoffensive term. Also twirp.

Twinkle: A term of endearment or form of address.

Twinnie: Affectionate term for a twin.

Twisting: A telling off, a scolding, a reprimand.

Twit: An idiot.

Twitcher: A bird watcher, an ornithologist.

Twocker: A person who steals vehicles. Also spelt twoc-er.

Twonk: A fool, idiot.

Two ticks: A short time, a couple of moments.

Two-time: To be unfaithful to one's partner. E.g."He's been two-timing on his girlfriend for the last 6 months."

Twunt: An idiot, a fool. A combination of the words 'twat' and 'cunt'.

Tyke: 1. A person from Yorkshire, England.

2. A mischevious person, used in good humour.

U

U-ee:	A u-turn. A term used by drivers.
Umpteen	Many, a lot of. E.g."There was umpteen colours to choose from."
Uncle Dick:	Sick, unwell. Rhyming slang.
Uncle Ned:	1. The head. Rhyming slang.
	2. Bed. Rhyming slang.
Uncle Tom:	A black person.
Undercarriage:	The male or female genitals.
Undercrackers:	Underpants.
Underkecks:	Underpants.
Unhinged:	Insane, mentally unstable and unpredictable.
Uni:	Abb. of university.
Up	Intoxicated by drugs, high.
Upper:	A stimulant drug, usually amphetamine sulphate.
Up sticks:	To move on, to settle or live elsewhere.

V

Vadge:	Vagina.
Vagitarian:	Lesbian. A pun on vegetarian.
Varda	To look at. Mainly gay use and originating from Polari. Also varder, vardy, vada, and vardo.
Veggie:	Abb. of vegetarian.
Veg-out:	To vegetate, chill-out.
Vino	Cheap inferior wine.
Vinyl:	Gramophone records, not cds.
Voddy:	Vodka.
Vom:	Vomit.
	To vomit. E.g."I had gastric flu and felt like I was going to vom."

W

Wabs: Female breasts.

Wack: 1. A term of address.

2. Bad, wrong, worthless.

Wacko Crazy, insane.

Wack off: To masturbate. Also whack off. E.g."I wacked off with all my dad's stash of porn laid out in front of me."

Wacky: Crazy, zany.

Waffle: To talk aimlessly.

Aimless talk, nonsense.

Wag it /off: To play truant. Mainly adolescent use.

Wallies: False teeth.

Wally: 1. An idiot or imbecile. Prolific use during the early 1980s.

2. A pickled cucumber, a gherkin.

Wannabe: A person who aspires to be someone else, usually a celebrity and consequently imitates their life or image.

Wang: To throw.

Wanger: 1. A penis. Also spelt whanger.
2. An idiot.

Wank biscuit: A contemptible or objectionable person.

Wanker: 1. A masturbator.
2. A contemptible person.
3. An idiot, an incompetent person.

Wanking: Masturbation.

Wank mag: A pornographic magazine.

Wank pit: A bed.

Wankshaft: A contemptible person.

Wanksplat: A contemptible person or thing.

Wanky: Rubbish, of very poor quality.

Wap 1. A wasp. Also wappy.
2. A woman's breast. Usually in plural.

Wassock: An idiot, imbecile. Also 'wazzock'.

Watersports: The act of urinating on another for the sexual pleasure of both parties involved.

Way-out: Unusual, unconventional, avant garde.

Waxa Good, excellent. Adolescent usage, mainly.

Wazoo: The bottom, the anus, the rear end. Also, occasionally spelt wazzoo.

Wazzock:	An idiot, imbecile. Also 'wassock'.
Wazzocked:	Totally intoxicated by alcohol or drugs.
Weasel:	A despicable, usually sly and deceitful person.
Weasel-water:	A drink that is weak and insipid, often used with reference to tea.
Wedding tackle:	A euphemism fo the male genitals.
Wedge:	Money, usually implying a large amount.
Wee buns:	Easy, simple. Also weebuns.
Weepy:	A film that is sentimental and emotional.
Wee 'un:	A child or baby.
Wegie /Weegie:	A Glaswegian, a person from Glasgow.
Well gone:	Very intoxicated by alcohol or drugs.
Well hung:	Having a large penis.
Wellied:	Drunk, intoxicated.
Welly:	To kick forcefully.
Wellybobs:	Wellington boots.
Welly-gogs:	Wellington boots.
Wet:	Feeble, emotional, effeminate.
Wet blanket:	A miserable person unwilling to participate in an enjoyable event or moment.
Wet lettuce:	An emotionally weak person.

Wet nellie: A feebleminded person.

Whiffy: Smelling unpleasant.

Whinge: To persistently complain, in an irritating manner.

To act in the manner of the.

Whip: To steal. E.g."I had my wallet whipped last night."

Whoopsie: Excrement, a deposit of faeces. A generally puerile expression.

Wide: Self-assured, clever, sharp.

Widgy: Affectionate term for the penis.

Wife-beater: Stella Artois lager.

Willies: Nerves, worries, frights.

Willy: The penis. Generally humorous or affectionate usage.

Willy-woofter: A homosexual male.

Wimpy: Feeble, weak. Also applied to objects or places, e.g."The furnishings were a little wimpy for such bold decor."

Winch: To court, to date.

Winching: Courting, dating.

Windbag: Someone who talks incessantly.

Winkle: Affectionate name for a penis.

Winnits: Faecal remnants that adhere to the anal hairs. Also winnets.

Wino A habitual and often destitute drunkard.

Wiped out:	Exhausted.
Wired:	Stressed, nervy or anxious. Often with respect to having imbibed stimulants, such as cocaine or amphetamine.
Witch:	A despicable, nasty, or spiteful woman.
Witter on	To talk incessantly and superficially.
Wog:	A black/asian person. Offens.
Wolf:	To eat greedily or quickly. E.g."It's no wonder you have indigestion, wolfing your food that fast!"
Womb broom:	The penis.
Wombled:	Very intoxicated, by drink or drugs.
Wood / woody:	An erect penis.
Woolies:	Woolworths, the store.
Woolly:	A woollen jumper or cardigan.
Wop:	An Italian, or of Italy.
Word:	I agree!
Works:	The equipment necessary for an addict to inject drugs.
Wow:	To impress or excite. E.g."I've made up my mind to wow her with a bunch of flowers and an expensive meal."
Wrap	A tiny paper envelope for holding a quantity of illicit powdered drug.

Wreck: To hurt. E.g."My arm's wrecking - I think I fell badly last night when we were drunk and dancing."

Wrecked: Very intoxicated with alcohol or drugs.

Wupp To thoroughly beat. E.g."I'm going to wupp his ass if he tries that again."

X

X-rated: Lewd, obscene, pornographic. Taken from the now obsolete film classification rating..

X-ray eyes: Having the apparent ability to see through things.

XTC: Abb. of ecstasy (the pronunciation of), the drug MDMA.

Y

Yack up:	To vomit. E.g."That was the worst meal ever; I feel like yacking up."
Yacky:	Disgusting, vile.
Yam:	Home. Also 'yem'.
Yampy:	Crazy, mad, insane.
Yank:	An act of masturbation. Male usage. E.g."Oh God! I just walked in on Martin having a yank."
Yap	To talk incessantly.
Yard:	One's home.
Yardie:	A member of a Jamaican criminal gang. Usually operating internationally and in the distribution of illicit drugs.
Ya wank:	A contemptible person.
Yawn	Something that is very boring. E.g."Amanda's boyfriend is obsessed with football, he's such a yawn."
Y-bone steak:	The female genitals.
Yellow belly:	A person from Lincolnshire.

Yitney: A coward. Also yitni.

Yob: A lout or hooligan. Derived from the backslang of boy.

Yobbo Meaning the same as 'yob'.

Yomp To walk hard and with vigour.

Yonks: An age, a long time.

Yoursen: Pron. Yourself.

Yucky: Very unpleasant or distasteful.

Z

Zapper:	A TV remote control unit.
Zilch:	Nothing, zero.
Zip it:	Stop talking, shut up. Usually in the imperative.
Zit:	A spot, pimple or boil on the skin.
Zonked:	Worn out, tired. Also followed by out. E.g."Any chance we can have a rest? I can't go any further, I'm totally zonked."
Zoot:	A marijuana/cannabis cigarette, a 'joint'.
Z's:	Sleep, a nap. Pronounced zeds. E.g."I think i'll get some z's before we leave."
Zeds:	Sleep. E.g. "I really must get some zeds before we go out tonight".
Zeig heils:	Rhyming Slang for piles.

Bibliography

A.D. Peterkin, *Outbursts: A Queer Erotic Thesaurus,* Arsenal Pulp Press, Vancouver, 2003.

Bernard Share, *Slanguage - A Dictionary Of Irish Slang,* Gill and Macmillan, Dublin, 1997.

Chris Donald, *Roger's Profanisaurus,* John Brown Publishing Limited, London, 1998.

Chris Lewis, *A Dictionary Of Playground Slang,* Allison & Busby Ltd., London, 2003.

Eric Partridge, *A Dictionary Of Slang And Unconventional English,* Routledge and Kegan Paul, London, 1984.

Ewart James, *Ntc's Dictionary Of British Slang And Colloquial Expressions,* NTC Publishing Group, Chicago. 1997.

John Ayto, *The Oxford Dictionary Of Rhyming Slang,* Oxford University Press, Oxford, 2002.

Jonathon Green, *Cassell's Dictionary Of Slang,* Weidenfield & Nicholson, London, 2005.

______________, *Cassell's Rhyming Slang,* Cassell, London, 2000.

______________, *Slang Down The Ages,* Kyle Cathie Limited, 1994.

Julian Franklyn, *A Dictionary Of Rhyming Slang,* Routledge and Kegan Paul, London, 1975.

Michael Munro, *The Complete Patter,* Canongate Books, Edinburgh. 1998.

Michael Quinion, Port Out, *Starboard Home & Other Language Myths,* Penguin Books, London. 2004.

Paul Baker, *Fantabulosa - A Dictionary Of Polari And Gay Slang,* Continuum, London, 2002.

Ray Puxley, Fresh Rabbit, *A Dick'n'harry Of Contemporary Rhyming Slang*, Robson Books, London, 1998.

Tom Dalzell, *Flappers 2 Rappers - American Youth Slang*, Merriam-Webster, Springfield, Massachusetts. 1996.

_______________, *The Slang Of Sin*, Merriam-Webster, Springfield, Massachusetts. 1998.

Tony Thorne, *Dictionary Of Contemporary Slang*, Bloomsbury, London, 1997.